Stumbling Through the Undergrowth

the Undergrowth

An Approach to the Living of Life

Mark Kirwan-Hayhoe

Stumbling Through the Undergrowth

An Approach to the Living of Life

©1996 and 1999 Mark Kirwan-HEYHOE

ISBN 186163 077 8

First published 1997
Revised edition published 1999

Cover design by Paul Mason
Cover painting by Neil Geddes-Ward
The Dragon symbol is © 1995 Mark Kirwan-HEYHOE

Published by:

Capall Bann Publishing
Freshfields
Chieveley
Berks
RG20 8TF

This book is dedicated to

Hannah Madison Kimber

and to

Helen, Sarah and Sharon
for giving me such perfect moments in my life.

To Andrew —

Be well; be loved; be happy.

[signature] '00

Contents

Acknowledgements

The author gratefully acknowledges the assistance of Ms. Jacqueline Humphries and the Reverend Deborah Gray in the writing of this book. Their knowledge on matters religious and esoteric more than compensated for the author's own ignorance. The author would also like to thank Mr. Darren Garnett, whose knowledge of psychological theory proved invaluable, and Mr. Toby McCracken for his computer wizardry.

* * *

Who we are is partly formed by who we know. Others' opinions and beliefs permeate our own and it is through agreement or disagreement with them that our own ideas often become consolidated. Without the friendship, support, encouragement and *thoughts* of those I have known over the years, this book would not exist. It is thus with great respect that I acknowledge the following people, for they all, in one way or another (and sometimes in many), contributed to this book just by being who they are: Sharon Brine, John Dale, Iris de Carteret, David Graham, Deborah Gray, Sarah Kouhen, Joff Maxfield, Paul McCartney, Helen McConnell, Julie Poulain, Justin Scarlett, my philosophy tutor Dr. Claud Pehrson, my grandmother Ethel Medcalf, and Margaret and Ian Kirwan, my parents.

May all your dreams be as beautiful as you are.

Preface

Setting the Record Straight

It is said that the age of Aquarius is upon us. It is a time for spiritual matters, we are told, because (if nothing else) we are all going to die soon. Unlike the Fifties, when the world was going to end with an atomic bang, the world in the Nineties isn't going to end - just us. Whether through ozone depletion, pollution, mass infertility or fatal diseases, our time will soon be up. Well, maybe - but don't hold your breath. The oxygen's still out there.

In the run up to Aquarius, we have seen a phenomenal rise in New Age beliefs. People are desperately trying to find some solace, something to hold on to that gives them meaning. And, as with anything that says this is 'The Way', people expound that way by giving steps towards achieving it.

The belief system described in this book is not 'The Way'; it is just a way, one possible path. It is not meant to be seen as some sort of prescription; this particular spiritual approach is not being advocated above any other. It is simply the steps one person took in moving from sadness to calm, from anger to peace, from unhappiness to - if not happiness - at least a state of 'not-unhappiness'.

Many spiritual guides are written by people who seem to have reached the other end. They are books describing how you too can reach 'enlightenment'. Well, the author of this book is not some sort of spiritual guru, but a human being with faults and extremes and selfish desires who still gets angry and sad and lost and confused at times. Though much may have been learnt in the course of my spiritual journey, that journey is nowhere near completion. In fact, I have only just left the starting gate. Therefore, if this work is some kind of guide (in that there are things written down here which are felt to be truth), then remember that this guide could be the pompous ramblings of an egotistical man. What I believe to be truth may only be truth for me; if you do not feel it says truth to you, don't listen to it. All I am trying to do is offer a spiritual *smorgasbord*, a manual if you wish - and like any manual, you only use those sections that are relevant to your circumstances. So, take from it anything that appeals to you and leave behind the rest. And if none of it speaks any truth to you or does not suggest anything you did not already know to be truth, it is hoped at least that it focuses your thoughts for a while on the principles you follow - for it is good to consciously think about our beliefs at times, to remember what we hold most true.

After all, if not for principles, which stem from the belief that we can improve ourselves, you would not be reading this book, but wielding it as a club.

1: Towards a Definition of What It's All About

"Everything that can be said can be said clearly."

Ludwig Wittgenstein

1.

The Four Aspects of the Self

All spiritual paths have their own language. Whether Catholic or Celt, Hindu or Navajo, certain words and phrases have particular meanings other than the generally shared meaning we all use in everyday life. This is done because, by attaching certain meanings to those chosen words and phrases, an understanding of what is being said by one follower of a faith to another is achieved without lengthy exposition.

The spiritual path set out here is not an established faith. In fact, in the literal sense, it is not a faith at all. All it is is a combination of beliefs felt to be true; a way of looking at the world. No doubt, many of these beliefs are to be found in other faiths; indeed, subsequent study showed this to be so. What was intuitively felt to be truth was later found scattered across many existing creeds. Truth may indeed be subjective, but it seems that many have arrived at the same subjective truths. However, because this belief system is not an established path, particular phrases have been coined in an attempt to somehow convey with as few words as possible concepts that, if explained every time they were needed, would use a large number of words. Most are defined in their relevant places, but there are four phrases which need clarifying here, because they are at the very core of this path.

The foundation on which this belief system rests is that the essence of all of us is made up of four things: the head, the heart, the body and the spirit. The head is our rational side; the part of us that makes choices and decisions in a considered way. It is a long-term viewer. The heart is our emotional side; the part of us that makes choices and decisions from feeling. It is a short-term viewer. The body is our gratifier; the part of us that avoids pain and seeks pleasure. It is a short-term viewer that often thinks it is long. And the spirit is our will; the part of us that assimilates the events which occur to us and drives us onward. It is both a short- and long-term viewer. The word 'spirit' is not being used in this context to refer to spirituality, about what is believed or felt to be truth, nor is it a reference to the soul. Rather, it is the 'spirit' that is part of our essence, the vital force or *Self*, as it is called here - the core of what makes us us.

To put it another way, our actions and reactions to stimuli will be approached in the following ways by our four aspects. The head says 'I think', the heart says 'I feel', the body says 'I want', the spirit says 'I intend'.

However, these four aspects of our essence are not equal - and neither are they meant to be. We all lean towards one of these four aspects throughout our lives, and this aspect is the base on which the other three rest. It may be a head base, a heart base, a body base or a spirit base.

Head-based people tend to be thoughtful, inquiring, communicative; heart-based people are usually emotional, intuitive, sensitive; body-based people are often physical, practical, sensual; spirit-based people are, on the whole, multi-directional, passionate, forceful.

Some people use only one of these aspects throughout their lives. They have virtually shut off the other three. People who only use their head are cold, calculating, disconnected creatures. People who only use their heart are obsessive, compulsive and needy. People who only use their body are greedy, vain and superficial. People who only use their spirit are restless, insensitive and opinionated. These people are few and far between. Most of us use all four of our aspects, but we use them in a hierarchical way. We use our base the majority of the time, but allow that base to be influenced by our other three aspects. It is how much we allow one or all of these aspects to have a say that leads to the kind of person we are; how extreme or balanced our actions and reactions in this world will be.

However, many of us do not explicitly recognise the existence of all four aspects. We may, for example, be a spirit-based person who allows our head to have a say a lot and our body to have a say sometimes, but never consciously acknowledge our heart for what it is. It will only be due to a series of events, traumatic or otherwise, occurring to us - a series of events often known as a 'spiritual awakening' - that we become aware there are other aspects to our essence and actively try to develop those aspects and reduce the influence of our own base.

If we learn anything from the spiritual journey that follows this awareness, it is this: if we are to be whole, we must balance these four aspects of ourselves. Yes, it is good to have a base - but we should never let that base rule us to the exclusion of one or more of our other aspects. If we do, we will never move forward.

A major part of spiritual development is learning to balance these four aspects and in getting them to work as one as best we can. The more we listen to all four, the more accepting we become of life and our place in it. If this is achieved, the nearer we are to wholeness - and when that point is reached, life (in some undefinable way) becomes better in the living.

2.

The Correlation Between The Self & The Elements

The four aspects of the Self have corresponding Elements that go with them. The belief system presented here places head with Air, heart with Water, body with Earth and spirit with Fire[1] (it is important to remember that the spirit being referred to here is to do with behavioural patterns, not the higher Spirit that many faiths consider to be the Fifth Element). So, a head-based person is usually an Air person; like Air, they can be warm or cold, strong or gentle, whisper or howl, caress or flatten. A heart-based person is usually a Water person; like Water, they can be stagnant or flowing, deep or shallow, direct or meandering, troubled or calm. A body-based person is usually an Earth person; like Earth, they can be fertile or barren, solid or shifting, supportive or crushing. A spirit-based person is usually a Fire person; like Fire, they can be explosive or slow-burning, provide heat or scorch, rage or glow.

All Elements contain the positive and negative; they can all be creative or destructive. So can we.

There is nothing new here. From Astrology to Jung, links have always been made between the Elemental forces and our psychological make-up. There have been differences between these links since the ancient religions began to correlate the internal with the external, but almost all have worked within the same framework: one Element for each of our aspects.

There are always exceptions, of course, just as there are exceptions in astrology between star signs and their usual character definitions. Astrologers explain these differences through ascendencies, planet conjunctions, cusps, etc.: the reason why this Sagittarius does not behave like a typical Sagittarius is because so-and-so. The exceptions under the belief system described here are considered otherwise. The reason why a person seems to have an Elemental sign contradictory to the base aspect of their Self is either because that base is heavily influenced by another aspect of that Self, or - as is more usually the case - their upbringing and/or the experiences they have had in life has *changed* them. A heart-based person who has had their love abused time and again may become cold and harsh rather than warm and caring, for instance. Fear of being hurt alters their approach to relationships. They are no longer working from their base - their natural inclination and instinct - but from another aspect of their Self.

The balance of the base aspect of the Self and our other aspects - our base Element and the other Elements - explains the paradoxes we see in people's personalities. For example, a Fire or spirit-based person may be very passionate, but if that person has attempted to strike an internal balance, the passion will not always surface. When facing a problematic situation, the Fire base will immediately want to set light to it, forcing it to flare up until it has exploded or burnt itself out. Sometimes, though, this will not be the best approach; sometimes it is better to allow a gentle breeze to cool the situation down. A Fire person who has moved towards balance will recognise this; they will access their Air side, use their head, and act appropriately.

Of course, some are precisely the opposite. It is not balance that presents another side of them to the world, but internal conflict of the Self - contradictory behaviour rather than paradoxical. Elements can both negate each other and heighten each other's force. Air can blow out Fire or fan the flames; Fire can evaporate Water or bring it to the boil; Water can wash Earth away or nourish it; Earth can direct the movement of Air or smother it. It is when the Air caresses, the Fire warms, the Water the right temperature, the Earth fertile that the Self is balanced, the personality at peace.

– – –

1 As far as I am aware, under the definitions given, this model does not go against any Western or Eastern spiritual philosophies or psychologies except possibly the Tibetan Five Skandhas which places Earth with feeling, Water with awareness, Fire with perception, Air with will/intention and the body with a fifth element of Ether. However, my knowledge of Tibetan philosophy is shaky at best and it may well be that the understanding I have of the Five Skandhas is incorrect and there is no clash at all.

3.

The Four Types of Self

The four aspects of the Self are like a Venn diagram. All four aspects touch one another in different ways, and there is a centre where all four become one. This is the core within the Self; the core within the Core. It is the part of us that, when we access it, works best of all. When we tune into that core, we become what we truly are; we become balanced. In diagrammatic form, it looks like the figure opposite.

However, this Venn of our Self is neither unchangeable in its formation or its shape. We can make the overlaps bigger, alter the position of each part - and we can damage the circles. Similarly, though the shade, the tone of the Self - be it warm, cold or neutral - is marked in permanent ink when we are born, we can lighten or darken that tone or allow it to be modified by others' pens. Just as there are four aspects of Self, so there are four types of Self. Warm, Cold, Damaged and Inert.

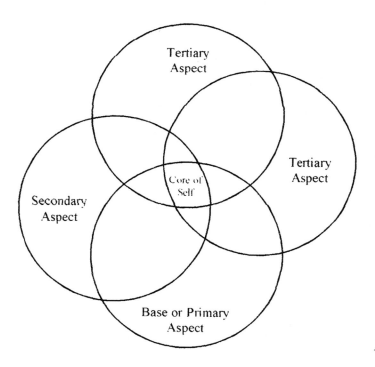

Fig. 1. The Venn of the Self

(i) Warm Selves and Cold Selves

It is one of the most fundamental wrongs in this life to actively encourage two people who are together to separate when those two people still feel love for each other. It is an even more fundamental wrong to work on one of these people to leave their partner and be with you. To influence and manipulate someone with the aim of destroying their existing partnership with another because you want a relationship with that person yourself is one of the great cardinal 'Do Nots'. To set out to crush the love between two people for your own gain - no matter how much you know they would be happier with you - means you will pay so heavily, it will be virtually impossible for you to make redemption, even if you do not succeed in crushing that love. And it is never done by Warm Selves, because a Warm Self would neither want the person they desire to ever feel resentment towards them for having left their former lover (selfish motive) or cause pain to anyone, even someone they did not know, who was hindering the progress of their love (selfless motive).[1]

A Cold Self would do it without even hesitating.

A Warm Self is a Self that rarely deliberately sets out to harm. They will do so at times, either through mistake or through imbalance of their four aspects, but these occasions are usually unintended. If they are spiritually aware, they know that when they do cause harm they will have to both pay for it and endeavour to make recompense in some form or another. That recompense may not be to the person or thing they harmed, but it will be done in some way to some other person or thing.

A Cold Self will harm anybody who is standing between them and what they want.

Warm Selves do not always have their own gain at the top of the agenda; Cold Selves rarely have anything else. A Warm Self does not destroy; a Cold Self does - and not only for personal benefit. They also do it for pleasure; for the sense of power it gives them.

The example of destroying a relationship was used because it points out a founding principle of the path set out here - that there are certain actions you do not make, even if it is advantageous for others as well as yourself, if in the course of that action, *a third party is harmed*. Not only should you avoid harming others directly, you should also avoid harming others indirectly if you are aware of that potential indirect harm. Direct harm may sometimes be needed to be done (physical restraint toward someone in order to stop them inflicting violence on yourself or others, for example), but indirect harm should be avoided. If it is indirect, it means there is another person between yourself and the one to be harmed. It should be that other person's choice of action as to whether harm occurs or not, not yours. One does not have the right to influence or make a decision for another; one should only give opinions or options if requested. What is done with those options or opinions - accept or reject, consider or ignore - is up to the person who has requested it.

(ii) Damaged Selves

Damaged Selves do harm when they think they are doing good. Damaged Selves destroy when they are trying to create. Damaged Selves hurt themselves and those they love around them. Damaged Selves do the wrong things for the right reasons - and then, when they realise they have done wrong, they deny they did it.

The more you deny a wrong, the more you will pay for doing that wrong.

However, Damaged Selves do not pay as heavily as Cold Selves for the wrongs they do, as it is not entirely their fault. If you are nowhere near to being whole in this world, no matter how spiritually developed you are, how can you possibly be punished fully for the wrongs you commit? If someone has a broken leg, how can they be expected to walk properly? If they knock over another person while walking on the street, they are not entirely to blame. They are partly in error - if they had not tried to put weight on that leg, they would not have sent the passer-by crashing to the ground - but they did not mean to do it. They did not deliberately break their leg; that was done to them against their will.

Some Damaged Selves refuse to admit their leg is broken, though - and in that refusal, they fail to let it heal properly. The leg may become strong again, but it is bent and out of shape. For those of us who know these Damaged Selves, we should encourage them to have the leg reset, but we cannot force them. They have to decide for themselves. All we can do is say we will provide the crutches and nurse them while the leg heals properly. And, if you are close to them, you may have to set the leg yourself or with the help of the others.

As to the reasons why that Self got damaged, there can be a few or so many - emotional torment, constant physical pain, mental illness, stress at work or home, violent or sexual abuse, feeling of failure, bad parenting, rejection. Sometimes, it is easier to list the reasons that did not do damage - but the result is the same. The Damaged Self cannot, in their damaged state, function properly; they do not have the wherewithal to ever become whole; they will be unbalanced and so not be using all four of their aspects properly. Sometimes, this will appear in the form of too great a leaning on their base to the exclusion of the others, resulting in extremist actions. At other times, this will appear as a careering from aspect to aspect - from head to heart to spirit to body, and every variable within - resulting in confusion. The third variation is that they use the wrong aspect as their base, resulting in unhappiness and insecurity.

Sometimes, they will do all three. These are the most Damaged Selves of all. If this is the case, the chances are an attempt to repair the damage will be met with rejection. But one of our specific roles in life is to offer support if it is needed. Whether that offer is accepted or not is irrelevant. We have to leave the door open to allow them to knock and enter. We have to have the crutches ready, to know how to set the leg, if they ask for help. We have to try.

However, we are not solely what we come from; we are not entirely the result of what we have experienced - we are also what we make ourselves. The awareness of what has been done to us should doubly protect us from using it in the same way (having been hurt and not wanting to hurt another). If this is not done, it shows the amount of damage caused. The more the damage, the more we protect ourselves from further damage by damaging others first. We stop working from our true base; we deceive ourselves into thinking the base we use is the one we should use, and so we become very deceitful in our life to ourselves and others. So many false promises given which we believe we can fulfil; so many delusions reiterated so that others come to believe in them and ourselves; so many half-truths told as full truth; so much trust abused and broken. We hurt people, some of them very badly, who are close to us. Most of those people will then leave us.

Each time a Damaged Self does this, each time they push or drive someone away, they lose another chance to get it right, another chance to move towards wholeness. Eventually, they run out of chances. They are too damaged to do it by themselves and will not ask for help, will not even accept the fact that they are damaged. We must all face our demons and deal with them; the longer we refuse to look at them, the harder it is for us to rip them out. Like a swimmer who is using the back stroke to win a race when their strongest stroke is the front crawl, the Damaged Self may win for so long - but eventually they will be beaten.

Damaged Selves do not get many offers of crutches. The more they reject those offers, the less offers are made, until they have pushed away everyone who got too close to them, for fear of being seen for what they are: not whole. They never seem to realise (or refuse to accept) that often those close to them - their partners and good friends - already recognise that incompleteness and only want to help them grow. Which is why there are so many lonely people.

We are all damaged in one way or another, even Cold Selves (how Cold a Cold Self is depends much on how they deal with the hurt inflicted on them during their life). The question is, how much are we aware of that damage, how much of that damage will we admit to ourselves, and what are we prepared to do about it. The less we do, the lonelier we will become. If we cannot face ourselves, cannot admit to ourselves our incompleteness, refuse to be aware of our self-deceptions, then we will never let others get near enough to us, never allow total intimacy to occur. If we do not work on our own feelings of worthlessness, our lack of self-esteem; if we do not share our fears of Self, then we will lose or throw away those who love us. We will end up lonely and bitter and alone, unless we are with someone who just does not care - in which case we will still be lonely, for not being cared about is to be lonely. This person may be a Great Love to us now, but if we do not repair our damage they will not stay that way. They will just become someone we live with, not someone who is part of us. And that is not the aim.

(iii) Inert Selves

Inert Selves are a rarity. They are often superficial, will adapt to almost any situation, can mingle with almost anyone. They go through life quite merrily, hardly feeling the blows and enjoying the pleasures, with little thought of why they are doing it. Inert Selves have few genuine deep-seated beliefs, even if they profess otherwise; their principles are often changing and you never seem able to quite work out what makes them tick. The reason is because there is no mechanism ticking. They just exist - a human Winnie-the-Pooh who has occasional bad moods. They often disappear in times of crisis; if you have a problem, they will not be there to help. And Inert Selves create one other response in you. You cannot help but like them. They are charming, pleasant and fun to be with - if a little irritating in their selfishness.

Inert Selves are new souls. They go through life never quite getting a grip on it, almost as if it is a practice run, which - if they are a new soul - it is. They are just starting out on the many lifetimes they will live. They can be very happy, but they do not think about the questions of life a lot. Who am I? Where am I going? What is my purpose? These questions do not crop up in their minds a great deal; they just flit across from time to time. Which is not to say they have no spirituality. Indeed, there are Inert Selves who try to access their spirituality a great deal. This year they may be reading Castenada and experimenting with consciousness-altering drugs. The next, they may well be Earth-worshipping or pursuing trans-cendental meditation. None of it will really work, for they are doing it for the wrong reasons. They want to find out how they can benefit from these pursuits - what they can personally gain - not how they can benefit all.

If all this sounds patronising, it is. Inert Selves are true beginners. They have to be left alone to get on with it. If they ask for your opinion or advice, then give it. They will almost certainly ignore it, but at least they asked. Just smile wryly and let them continue. Someone can only be guided after they have become spiritually aware; no-one can place that awareness in them. They have to make their own mistakes and accomplishments; they have to find the way onto the path by themselves. Everyone does eventually.

- - -

1 It may be that it is also wrong to be with someone who desires more than one relationship or who wishes to end a relationship they are in. It may be wrong to be a catalyst for them to leave that other person. Moral philosophers can make these decisions; the path followed here only gives general tenets. Individual circumstances are left to the individual to make their own rulings. Under this belief system, as long as you do not attempt to encourage a separation, do not seek to harm, you have not transgressed greatly. However, one question does come to mind. Would you like your partner to have a relationship with somebody else? If the answer is no, then perhaps you should refrain from having a relationship with someone who already has a partner, for that partner may feel the same way as you.

4.

The Four (Suggested) Aims of Life

Whilst defining Inert Selves, the word 'lifetimes' was mentioned. This is due to the belief that we live multiple lives - in Buddhist terms, that we are on a cycle of birth, death and rebirth. However, unlike Buddhism, the belief system presented here does not view this cycle as circular.

Many religions see our spiritual life in terms of a circle or wheel (the ladder is another well-known symbol, but it tends to be used by faiths which hold that we live one life only). We go from this world to the next - which does not have to be a world or worlds for everyone; it can be a higher plane or level of consciousness or whatever - and back again until we have finally paid off all our debts and led as good a life as we can. Yet in many ways, this image seems spiritually to be lacking somewhat.[1]

Early on in spiritual development, almost all of us become aware that the living of a life in this world, the being in the next, the living of a life in this world, etc. is 'spiralistic', not circular.[2] In scientific terms, it is helicoidal. Nature moves from one season to another, but that motion is not circular - we just see it as such. Plants may live, release their seeds and die, and their seeds form new plants, but those new plants are at liberty to evolve. They can change. And so can we, and so we do. As each life we live in this world ends, we have either moved up the spiral or moved down, but we have not gone round in a circle - for a circle suggests there is no end. A circular path does not finish where we step off it. A helicoidal path does; there is an end to a spiral. In fact, there are two ends: one at the bottom, the other at the top.

This is not a movement toward the concept of Heaven and Hell. The belief system set out here does not include the possibility of descending into fiery pits to have molten lava poured over us for all eternity. There is a belief in transgression and payment - a spiritual equivalent of crime and punishment, if you will - but those who transgress constantly life after life do not eventually descend to the bottom of the spiral to fall off into some tortuous underworld. Those who do fail, who do find themselves at the bottom, are simply stuck there until they start living lives in which they do more good than harm and begin climbing. When we die, the 'good' do not go to one place while the 'bad' to another. There may be different levels or tiers; there may be Overworld and Underworld - but they are all part of one. We all go to the same. It is just that, while there, we learn how well we are doing - and, of course, face the (hopefully good-humoured!) wrath of those we transgressed against who are waiting for us. The Otherworld may be a Paradise, but if it is it may well be a Paradise of sorts, as pleasant or unpleasant, uplifting or humbling, as we deserve. The less transgressions, the more comfortable we are allowed to feel, the more enjoyable our stay until we go back to live another life in this world. Furthermore, whatever the Otherworld is, it is unlikely to be a rest home; there will be work to do there too and perhaps mistakes can still be made.

Eventually, if we work at it hard enough and finally lead as good a life as we can, we reach the top of the spiral. When that is done, we leave the spiral behind and stay in the Otherworld. And then our spiritual path has ended. We have reached our destination.

The belief in multiple lives leads to the conclusion that there must be reasons why we live life after life. Different faiths have different answers to this question. Here, that answer is threefold. We go through this process to achieve balance and wholeness, to seek resolution - and to fulfil a role.

Each time we live a life in this world, we are given a role. We may play many different parts in the lives of the people we meet, but we have one substantial role to perform. That role can vary from life to life, and there are an enormous variety of roles that could be given to us as we begin each new life, but we only have one main one for each life.[3] It could be that of an Arbitrator, a Carer, a Creator, an Empath, an Entertainer, a Guide, a Healer, an Inspirer, a Leader, an Oracle, a Sage, a Shaman or any number of a myriad other roles.

Whatever spiritual path we take, we should allow ourselves to be told our role. That telling may be a long time coming, but once you are aware you do have a role of some sort (an awareness that is known consciously when you begin to awaken spiritually), you will realise what it is at some point.

If you are still waiting to discover it, it may be that you have to be in a position to enact that role and are not there yet. It may be that you are already enacting that role, but will not recognise it for what it is until you have been doing it for a while. It may be that some people learn early and others learn late.

The list of possible roles is vast, but we do not get a choice from that list. Our role is set, and though it is fine to try out a variety of roles in the hope you will discover what your purpose in this life is, it is a mistake to decide 'this is my role', to label yourself as one particular thing. In so doing, you may have chosen wrong - and spend months, maybe years failing both at what you are trying to do and in fulfilling your true role.

Sometimes we try our best at the *wrong thing*. If you think you know what your role is, if you believe you have received that information, remember that we can get the messages confused, that jokers play tricks on us. Use your intuition; sit and wait awhile. Often, it is only after a period of waiting, of not trying to play any role, that we begin to get a hint as to what our role is. And it may well be others who tell you it, not yourself.[4]

In being aware that we have a role, in having a desire to be told that role, in showing the willingness to enact that role, we take another small step forward up the spiral. And if that role turns out to be one which causes us pain; if, in doing it, we know we will hurt ourselves, then we have travelled a long way up the spiral already in previous lives, because the higher up the spiral you go - to a point - the more each life in this world becomes a life in which you harm few, but are harmed.

At first glance, this could be interpreted to mean that the final time around is one where you harm no-one and are harmed greatly, have a very sad life and so be allowed not to experience it again. Indeed, there are people who fix in their own mind that their final time on this world (which, unsurprisingly, they usually believe is the one they are presently living) will be one full of sadness and·pain, but will also be one in which they advance to the height of their faith. In this way, they believe, they will end their life lonely and alone, having been hurt greatly throughout it, hurt others as little as possible (and paying dearly for it during their life when they did)[5] - but spiritually, they will be enriched. Having, at the end of their physical life, paid their dues and followed their path without compromise, they will have reached the top of the spiral and thus end the cycle of birth and rebirth.

However, this is not so; indeed, nothing could be further from the truth. Yes, we do spend a time on the spiral where we are hurt greatly but hurt others little - but this is not the final part of the journey. To reach the top of the spiral, you have to move towards wholeness, and this is the key. The more balanced a life you lead, the wholer that life is - both in terms of the balance you create within you between your head, your heart, your body, your spirit *and* in terms of what you do and what is done to you - the higher up the spiral you go. The aim of each life is to be as whole as possible during it. When you finally achieve this as best as can be done, when you balance the four parts of you inside yourself, when you harm no-one and few harm you, do good and receive good and so have a very happy life, then you will be allowed to finally leave this world - and you will leave it totally at peace. The last life you live is not the worst. It is the best.

It does not matter how spiritually fulfilled and developed you are at the end of a life; it does not matter how little you hurt but were hurt. What matters is how whole you were when you lived that life. An example. If you had balanced your spirit side with your head and body, but constantly refused to allow your heart to develop - if, when making choices, you used your head, body and spirit to make those choices, but switched off your heart completely while doing so - you have about as much chance of not being reborn into this world (no matter how much you believe otherwise) as I have of winning the Nobel Peace Prize. *It will not happen.*

Wholeness can be achieved in different ways. It is done both internally, through the conscious effort to use the four aspects of the Self in a balanced manner, and externally, through the use of those four aspects in our interactions with the world. Much of that interaction is done with other people; some of those people we have known before.

Just as we live more than one life, so we meet the same people over and over in those lives. Their bodies change, their Selves alter, but it is the same soul. There are some people who we are linked to; people whom we harm or help, hurt or make happy - and they do the same to us. It is our connections to these souls that play a large part in our movement up or down the spiral. Get it right, we move up; get it wrong, we move down.

The aim is to resolve with these souls - to either heal a hurt caused in this lifetime, to live a life in which no hurt occurs or to make recompense through love and care transgressions you made against them in previous lives. This is not a straightforward task. Pain is so easily given, so simple to inflict. What seems to be a soft blow to you may be a razor blade to them. Love and care, on the other hand, take time to build; they are slow processes which may take years to cultivate before their fruition.

Furthermore, one has to step cautiously between the interaction with the souls you know and their knowing of each other. To progress with one soul you may harm another. So many souls who constantly meet in lifetime after lifetime do so as friends and lovers, and often are both in the same lifetime. To leave one lover for another, to have split loyalties between friends, are situations fraught with danger. Like the mountain climber, there are only so many ways of ascending the cliff face; choose the wrong hand or footholds and your errors cause harm to both yourself and others.

Each life we live is not directed entirely by choice. There are souls you are destined to meet. Move from one place to another, one job to another; change the course of your life as much as you wish - there will be other souls waiting for you and souls you left behind who you will see again. The souls we are linked to are an extended group. Fate's subtle machinations bring us together. We may not meet all of them in each given life, but we do connect with a goodly amount - and the more of these souls we make resolution with, the more we heal the wounds until there is only love and understanding between the two of you (whether as lovers, ex-lovers, family or friends), the less souls we have to continue resolving with. The higher up the spiral we have gone.[6]

With a spiritual awakening there may come an awareness that certain people we know we have met before in previous lives. We may not be sure of them all, but there will be this knowledge of some. This awareness may not come to all of us; it all depends on how old a soul we are. Newer souls have less cognition and are thus less able to recognise. However, no matter how new our own soul is, with a spiritual awakening comes the knowledge that we do meet certain souls time and time again, even if that knowledge is not consciously recognised. As long as we remember that one of the goals in our life is to cause as little hurt as possible, we will endeavour not to transgress against others and so are less likely to inflict pain on other souls, whether known in previous lives or not.

As new people come into our lives, there will be some who we have an instant liking for, an attraction, a connection. We will want to sustain that connection. Chances are they are souls we have met before. Occasionally, we meet people in fleeting; *frisson* occurs, there is a feeling of warmth. Do not let these people walk away without an attempt to connect; they may be souls we have known previously. Let them pass and it is an opportunity to resolve wasted.[7]

Some of the souls we meet we may hurt badly; some may hurt us. Either way, we should keep the connection; should try to resolve. We should try to make up for the pain we have caused; should accept and forgive those who have caused us great pain - especially when we remember that the pain dealt to us is payment for transgressions previously done by us (either in this or a previous life) and those who have hurt us will have to suffer their own payment too. There could be souls who are our Nemesis - a person who causes us hurt time and time again, life after life - but we have to accept that and try to resolve anyway.[8] Even if we fail in the attempt, at least we genuinely tried. In that trying alone, we move up the spiral.

Our cycle of birth and rebirth does not end until resolution has occurred with everyone we have to resolve with - but during each life, we may find it cannot be done with some, that there are people who will not allow us to resolve. This may be due to their own failing, but sometimes our transgression against them was just too great.

We may wish and strive for resolution, but we will not be successful. This means that, no matter how close we are to the top of the spiral, we have to come back until resolution (of a different sort in a different life) is made to *their* satisfaction. We do not step off the spiral, we are released; the ties that bind us have to be cut by others' hands.

It could be argued that these others cannot bring us back forever. If you have reached the top of the spiral in every other way, surely there comes a time where your transgression against them in a previous life is outweighed by their repeated refusal to allow resolution to occur. Surely the ties that bind do weaken. However, perhaps the whole point is that this is never needed. Resolution *always* occurs, in one life or another - because it is these final resolutions which *allow* us to reach the top. They are the final steps left to take. Balance, wholeness and the fulfilling of a role may move us up the spiral, but it is resolution that gets us to the apex.

The spiritual path described here is grounded in these four beliefs and aims - that we are given one main role in each life which we should enact; that the reliving of lives is a helicoidal process which we should endeavour to climb; that the resolution between ourselves and those we meet throughout all the lives we live is essential if we are to reach the top of that spiral; and that we should strive to be as whole and balanced as possible.

The odds are equal. The very first life we lived was not one that started at the bottom of the spiral. We must begin half-way up, because we have the capacity to do wrong, to harm, to destroy, just as we have the capacity to do good, to heal, to create. If we started at the bottom of the spiral in our first life, how could we go down any further if we transgressed? We cannot descend to a non-existent level.

Similarly, we cannot start our first life at the top of the spiral, because we learn from doing wrong or having wrong done to us, and it is from these wrongs - from these steps back - that we learn what is right and enact it, thus moving forward.

If we started at the top of the spiral, it would mean that whatever wrongs we do could never be overcome; we could never take enough steps forward to compensate and overreach the steps taken back. We would always be travelling down the spiral; the good we do would only slow that descent. Yet we know we can get better, we can become wholer. We can end a life having done more good than harm, and therefore reached a point higher up the spiral than the point at which we started that life. All that is left, then, is a first life that starts in the middle of the spiral - for if all lives are about balance, there must be balance to begin with. The mid-point of the spiral is that balancing point. The weight is equally distributed on either side.

Perhaps it is true, as many believe, that our path is already fixed; that it has been determined before we were born how we are going to live our lives. Perhaps Fate does rule us, not ourselves. But even if that is true, we do make choices. We do reach points in our lives where we decide how our lives will continue from that point. We are given alternatives and we choose one. Even if we are controlled by Fate, there is choice within that Fate. If that is not true, then there is no point in us doing anything; there is no point in us striving to improve the way we live our lives. If it is already fixed - if Doris Day was right when she sang 'Que Sera Sera' - we might as well go out and do whatever we want, hurt whoever we like, destroy everything we wish. We have that negative potential. Yet so many of us do not do this. We do try to improve, we do try to resolve, we do make sacrifices so that others can benefit. If we have the choice between good and bad, wrong and right - and we do because we have all chosen

38

to do wrong rather than right (and visa versa) at different times in our lives - then Fate cannot be in control. At the very most, it can only set the parameters. What we do within those parameters is up to us.

Sometimes, though, the parameters seem very tight - because sometimes, even if we rarely see it until later, the only way to move up the spiral is to move down it first. We have to take two small steps back to make one large step forward. That is what many of us do throughout our lives; we just do not realise it until a spiritual awakening. We have to hurt, be hurt and then not hurt in order to move further upward. How can we understand the pain someone would feel - and so choose not to inflict it - unless we have felt that pain; how can we know the sorrow someone is suffering for causing harm to another (either because of their awareness of having done wrong or because of the knowledge they have done right, but in doing so they have caused harm to someone else) unless we too have known that sorrow.

To take two small steps back hurts - partly because those small steps do not seem small at the time. Even when we take that giant step forward, it may not seem as if it was worth it in comparison - but then, we are the last to know where we are on that spiral, so who are we to judge?

– – –

1 I later learnt that at least one religion - Hinduism - in fact uses the spiral as a dominant image in their teachings, but unfortunately I did not come across this at the time of initial study. Other notable exceptions include the Axis Mundi, the Tau Cross (or Tree of Knowledge) and Bunyan's pilgrim's progress to the Celestial City.

2 It is not for one moment being suggested that Buddhism and other religions literally believe that reincarnation is a circular process. All that is being stated is that the image of the circle - a simple metaphor to describe the concept of birth, death and rebirth - is in fact too simplistic. A spiral seems to be a more effective image; a metaphor closer to the truth.

3 Of course, we are all given a particular role to make certain people happy. As far as that happiness is concerned, those close to us (whether they be lovers, family or friends) should find happiness either through what we do and how we are with them, or through what they do for us. The feelings of being useful, helpful, supportive or loving are some of the best in this world. To know you are needed or wanted by another gives the greatest satisfaction and pleasure.

4 Sometimes, the last voice we hear is our own - but sometimes it is the only voice we hear. Waiting for your role leads to another lesson: when to listen to others more than yourself.

5 Observation and experience have led to the conclusion, however, that those who approach life in this way - those who are striving for a self-fulfilling prophesy, in other words - do cause substantial harm to others in the process. Those who believe they will be greatly hurt arrange it so they will be greatly hurt. In that arrangement, others may suffer much also.

6 This does not mean we will never meet those souls again, merely that there will be no conflict. Once resolution is done, it is done.

7 However, do not restrain them either. You are trying to connect, not frighten. If they do not want to continue the

meeting, they are not ready to resolve with you - so let them go. You will come across them again if it is meant to be so.

8 Remember too that we may be a Nemesis for another (a further reason for causing as little harm as possible in this life we are living). And also consider that maybe, just maybe, there is an opposite of a Nemesis in our lives - a Nurturer if you will; someone who always gives us love and support, no matter what we do.

5.

The Four Combinations of the Soul

In previous chapters, reference was made to the notion of the soul and that some souls are old and others new. The soul is a problematic concept. Whole texts have been written on it and nothing else, but there is still no general concurrence as to what the soul is (and never will be; even if they do neurologically 'find' the soul, as is being attempted, it still will not explain what the soul consists of other than in terms of matter).

The quandary of the soul is, furthermore, complicated by the ideas of 'good' and 'bad'. To say one has a good soul or a bad soul says much, but what precisely is it saying?

Nothing in itself is good or bad. It is how we see it that makes it so. A mass murderer is not bad per se; it is our belief that murder is wrong that leads us to view them in this way. Therefore, any definitions of good and bad will be subjective. It is personal judgement, a value system, that places actions and reactions in one of these two categories. If you think it is bad, it is bad; if you think it is good, it is good. The fact that the rest of the world may agree with you in that placement is, ultimately, of no consequence. In this world, only logic is objective. Moral conclusions are subjective conclusions, no matter how many are in accordance.

This is not an advocation of Do What Thou Wilt Regardless, however. There is an objective idea of 'good' and 'bad'; it is just that we do not possess it. But to say *homo sapiens* may be unable to objectively judge what is wrong or right is not to say that higher authorities (or the Powers That Be as they are called here) cannot. You may not think you have wronged; the rest of the world may agree with you - but that does not mean you are correct. Our own history shows this: slavery, for example. At one point, virtually the entire Western world (and a substantial proportion of non-Western societies) believed slavery was acceptable. The dissenters did not even reach triple figures in number. Yet now it is considered by the vast majority of the population that slavery is wrong. Time has altered an entire planet's moral perception. The dissenters have become the norm.

The feeling of whether your soul is 'good' or 'bad' (always bearing in mind that the soul itself is neither, but what has been placed within it) comes with a spiritual awakening. In that moment, you are granted an objective understanding of 'goodness' and 'badness'. After that, you have a knowledge of your soul's presence, but not the objectivity. Good and bad become subjective once again. So, the references to good and bad souls made below are references to the objective 'good' and 'bad' that none of us can define. However, any examples given must by nature be subjective. We are unable to give any other.

* * *

With a spiritual awakening, we become truly aware that there are forces at work far greater than any power on this world; that there are patterns in everything we do; that there is a purpose to our lives other than our own purposes; that the life almost all of us are living is not the first and most certainly not the last. But we also receive something else. We are allowed a glimpse into our own soul and, like the figures in Plato's cave, we realise we had been previously seeing shadows.

We do not often see into our soul; we may not even recognise it for what it is when we do. Soul and Self can be confused. Perhaps the clearest definition that can be given is that Self is the *gestalt* of our four aspects, while the soul is that part of us which contains all our lives and sits within the Self.[1] It is a history book. It contains all we are, all we have experienced, all we have felt... and all that we have done.

To get a fleeting glimpse of our soul is supposed to be a wonderful experience. Perhaps this is true for those who have good souls. Perhaps their glimpses are ones of glory, but for others, this is not so. They too may have had glimpses of glory, but they were not glimpses within. Some souls do not contain a pleasant history; the past lives lived have not been exemplary.

The awakening we have, the awareness of things around us on a different level, can be accompanied with a feeling of sadness as well as joy. That sadness will be due to the revealing of a soul which is bad, because that exposure tells you you have a lot of work to do. No nearing the top of the spiral here; no old soul who has almost completed the cycle. Many of us are quite young and our souls are in a mess. We may care in this life; in past lives, however, we have been cruel. One can have a Warm Self and a bad soul, a Cold Self and a good soul. This not a contradiction. Self can change from life to life; the soul merely gets more added to it.

44

Like any history book, the soul contains good deeds and bad deeds. Honour and sacrifice are placed side by side with selfishness and betrayal. The more good an individual has done in their lives, the higher up the spiral they are, the better their soul is and visa versa. However, it is up to that individual as to whether they will do good or bad, be kind or cruel, love or hate, etc. An old soul can be good or bad, a new soul likewise, but that does not mean we have to continue this pattern. The choices are ours. We may be granted a particular beginning with each new life, but what we do after that is our responsibility. We live the lives; we make the decisions on the whole. The Powers That Be may direct us to play a particular role in others' lives from time to time, but again it is ultimately our choices that have led us to be put into that role. If we have not been treacherous in our life so far, for example, the Powers That Be will not manipulate us into being treacherous towards someone in order for that someone to make payment for a transgression of their own. We have to have shown an inclination for treachery in our life up to that point for us to be used in that way.

To have a bad soul does not allow you to advocate responsibility, just as belief in a faith should not allow you to advocate responsibility.

The glimpses we have into our souls do not show specific examples of what we have done in previous lives. Rather, it gives us *resonance* of what we have done. It shows the figure at the bottom of the balance sheet. Those in the black will feel joy; those in the red will not. However, with a spiritual awakening comes an acceptance that what we have to pay for we have to pay for. All we can do is accept that payment with grace and hope it will not be too painful - and if it is, we have to grit our teeth, feel that pain and take every chance we get to move the balance sheet into the black. We should not allow the pain meted out against us to corrupt the intention and potential we have to do good and continue doing good. We must not become what we behold. We should never allow those who hurt us to influence us by their actions into hurting them back or directing that hurt at others. No revenge; no unjust justification. Just acceptance and a moving on - hopefully with the knowledge of how to protect ourselves from a repetition of that hurt occurring to us again, for this is one of the ways we grow stronger and wholer. We should try to forgive; otherwise we become bitter and twisted, hateful and hurtful, selfish and thoughtless, closed rather than open. We should not shut part of ourselves down so that we cannot be hurt; rather develop the ability to recognise the warning signs and so avoid the hurt. Instead of building walls around our vulnerable points so that no-one can get in, dig moats and construct drawbridges. In this way, we allow ourselves to remain open enough to receive the joy that may be offered to us.

For those of us who have discovered we have bad souls, to not build walls is difficult. We will still get angry over things done to us; we will still feel the desire for revenge; we may still wish to lash out at others in our own pain; we may still not forgive all those who have hurt us. But we hope that one day we can evolve enough to let go of these feelings, to learn to forgive - and in so doing, cleanse our souls a little, put figures into the plus column, move towards the black and slowly turn the bad soul into a good soul. We can but try.

We are human and we are individuals. As humans, we have certain faults and as individuals, we have a certain combination of faults. Greed, selfishness, thought-lessness, callousness, pretentiousness, insensitivity - the list can be long. We do not want to use them, but we do nonetheless. It is hard to keep these negative aspects of ourselves at bay; they jump out of us at times. Even if invested with a Warm Self, it is natural at times to be harmful rather than helpful. To the people we care about we try to be good; to the world in general we can be bad. But we do not have to be.

This realisation that we can be good rather than bad, the knowledge that we have the capacity to try and the potential to succeed in that trying, is part of any spiritual awareness. Virtually every religion and faith agree on this point, for an obvious reason. It is not just about being good to others, it is also about being good to ourselves *by* being good to others. I help myself in helping you; you help yourself by helping me. Spiritual growth is in part a selfish growth. It is perhaps the only selfish thing we do that is positive.[2]

The four combinations of the soul - old/good, new/good, old/bad, new/bad - determine to an extent how much internal conflict we will face as we live our life, but ultimately it does not matter what kind of soul you have, good or bad; we all opt for the bad at times. Even the best of us can be greedy and selfish, hurtful and destructive. As we step through the forest of life, we will trip over the mess of roots and undergrowth - and sometimes we do so deliberately. Whichever, having fallen down, we must expect our knees to be bruised and our ankles to be twisted and accept that pain for what it is: payment for not looking or thinking more carefully before taking the step that sent us sprawling. The trick is to learn from each fall and be more prudent next time.

– – –

1 To use the analogy of the Venn diagram again, imagine Self as a two-dimensional image on paper. The soul is in the middle of that diagram - but it is three-dimensional.

We rarely see it, because, in this analogy, we cannot see in three dimensions. Occasionally, we are allowed to see that third dimension. It is then that we glimpse our soul. Another approach: imagine the Venn diagram of the Self standing vertically. The soul is what props it up. It 'sits' behind the Self.

2 If there is another, it is almost certainly our ability to love.

6.

Transgression & Payment; Beneficence & Reward

The belief system set out here is an altruistic system - but it is an altruism based partly on a non-altruistic premise. Goodness is not done purely in the desire to do good, the satisfaction of doing it, but because to deliberately not do good may result in our own suffering. It is not just a case of always wanting to do good, but also a case of not wanting to do bad. It is the fear of having to pay later for a selfish or hurtful act now. If we cause pain or hurt, the scales may have to be balanced; we will have to face pain, be given hurt. It is this fear of having those scales balanced, of having justice meted out to us, that stops us from doing harm. This belief in 'natural justice' - the system of transgression and payment, beneficence and reward that occurs during life - can be summed up in a single maxim.

What you do comes back to you.

You do good, you will benefit; you do harm, you will be harmed. Some of these acts will be returned in kind;

others will be very disparate to the act. A heart that is broken unfairly, a deception, an act of violence - these will result in the perpetrator's heart being broken unfairly, being deceived, having violence inflicted. . . but *only for some.* Someone who breaks a heart through selfish desire may have a heart that cannot be broken, for example. They do not feel love in a way that - if that love is removed - hurts them particularly, so the payment is felt by them in another form. A rapist may be caught and imprisoned, and he may be raped while in prison by other inmates, but in virtually any other scenario, a man cannot be raped. However, the rapist can be seriously punished in other ways.

Natural justice strives to repay in kind, but if that cannot be done, it will repay in the same area. Breaking a person's heart for no good reason is a heart transgression; if the person doing it has a hard heart in terms of loving people, they will lose something they do love. A rape is a head, heart, body and spirit transgression. The rapist can pay physically, emotionally, mentally and spiritually. And if repayment cannot be done in the same area, natural justice will repay in any way it can in this world. . . and perhaps in the next too.

There are patterns to natural justice, but those patterns are not always obvious. Some patterns are so subtle, so intricate in their detail, they may never be seen. Some transgressions result in immediate payment; others take years in the coming or even several lifetimes to complete. But unlike resolution, payment for transgressions manifest themselves in the same lifetime, especially if one is spiritually aware. It may not be an entire payment; it may continue through other lives - but the spiritually aware transgressor will recognise it for what it is. They will see the pattern.

50

Immediate payment of transgressions occur for small transgressions. You make a slight error and you pay for it quickly - a smack of the hand. Payment for larger transgressions take longer to emerge. We forget over time that it is due; it goes to the back of the mind. We fall into the trap of thinking it is safe to enter the water. And because a major transgression is not always paid for in the same way or even the same form, you cannot protect yourself from it because you do not know how it will manifest itself. That is the beauty of payment: what you do *does* comes back to you; you just never know how or when.

As with transgression and payment, so with beneficence and reward. And these rewards are as strong as the goodness done, as powerful as payments in their own way. The scales of generosity need to be balanced as much as the scales of wrongdoing. Even good that is done for primarily selfish reasons is rewarded. We get what we are worth; we receive what we deserve.

This is not a plea for sacrifice, however. Yes, at times personal sacrifice is worth doing and worth much. A small sacrifice can lead to much greater benefits for others; a large sacrifice even more so. But, under this belief system, balance is paramount. If you have a strong desire to be a Mother Theresa, then be a Mother Theresa. Part of the benefit you gain will be in fulfilling that desire. But if you have no desire to do such a thing, then do not do so. Unwilling sacrifice is pointless: you may be rewarded for it; you will move up the spiral - but an unwilling sacrifice means you may not achieve something else that was (or was going to be) asked of you. You may fail to fill another criteria. Your moving up in one way leads to a failure to move up even further in another.

Not all payments for transgressions finish with you. Indeed, very few do.[1] Payment and transgression is a continuous process, both individually and collectively. The debts we pay can have a terrible effect. It seems that, on the spiral, anyone chosen to be the agent of payment for a wrong you have done has to make their own payment for doing it. Like dominoes, we are all knocked down, one by one.

I transgress against you. Before I transgressed against you, you transgressed against someone else. They transgressed against another before that. In time I will pay for my transgression, and the person who transgresses against me will themself have to pay. Perhaps, as each new person does the transgressing, their payment is slightly less than the one before. Like an image being reflected, the more it reflects, the less sharp it becomes. Perhaps all the payments are equal in their pain. Perhaps it is variable (who has not felt that some payments were unduly excessive, while we got off lightly with others?). But many believe that the payment gets worse. As each new person transgresses against the one before in order for the one before to pay for their transgression, so the new transgressor has to pay even more. How much that payment is multiplied is hard to tell. There are some faiths which hold you pay threefold. This seems a little harsh when part of the transgression you do is occurring because the receiver has to pay for their own transgression - but then, just because we do not wish for people to suffer, do not want them to pay so much, does not mean it will not happen. We may be in part the agents of payment, but we do not control the amount being paid. We are the servants in this role, not the masters.

Payment by one person on another who has transgressed previously can be done without further transgression. A Warm Self, a wise soul, can achieve this. If it is done with honesty and gentleness and consideration - with an awareness of knowing you are going to hurt but not wanting it to hurt anymore than it has to - the payment is still made. The pain will be as devastating as the person who transgressed deserves. But if it is done deceitfully, thoughtlessly, selfishly, the recipient of payment suffers more than was required and the domino effect continues to occur.

Certain religions state that merit can be transferred. If this can be done, it seems reasonable that payment can be transferred too. Celtic lore has this principle; it contains the possibility of transferring payment. However, it also warns that to do this will compound the payment of the original transgressor. You cannot put your payment onto someone else forever; eventually you too pay - and that payment will be harsher because of your attempt to delay. In effect, you have transgressed in three ways: firstly, the original transgression; secondly, the transgression of avoiding your payment; thirdly, the transgression of causing someone else to suffer your payment for a while.

On learning this, it immediately confirmed what had previously felt right intuitively. You can transfer payment as well as virtue. There was a codicil though. Payment can only be transferred onto someone who is presently enacting the same kind of transgression. Just as a thief can be convicetd of a theft s/he did not actually commit, so a transgression can be 'shifted' onto another. However - and it is worth reiterating - this transference can never be permanent. No matter how powerful you are, if you have trans-gressed, you will pay for that transgression. The scales of justice will be balanced whether we like it or not. If we do not try to make amends ourselves, our payments will be forced upon us in a far more painful way than if we had made our own attempt. We must try to resolve with those we have hurt - and do so to their satisfaction. If we fail, we pay. But if we do not even attempt to try, our payment will be more severe.

The wrongs we do can echo previous wrongs we have done, both in this and in previous lives. As such, we can pay for those transgressions along with the transgression we have recently committed. This is why some payments seem so unfair; why the punishment seems more severe than the crime. No matter how much one person wrongs and the other is wronged; no matter how much one person is guilty and the other innocent, the victim has contributed too. They have contributed in that they have previously transgressed against another. However, once paid for, the payment is over. It may take several lifetimes, but when it is done it is done. Then it is time for the person delivering the payment to pay.[2]

Sometimes we not only pay for transgressions by direct harm, we also pay indirectly. We not only suffer pain being dealt to us, we also suffer from not receiving benefit we could have received. We may not even realise what it was we failed to gain (that we will learn in the Otherworld) - but even then, in some small part of our Self, we are occasionally startled with the realisation that something was missed. The shock that sometimes wakes us in the middle of the night which we know no reason for; the sudden loss we feel for something we never had; a melancholia that descends on us; a feeling of what might have been. These may not always be an unknown sound, an unfulfilled desire, a chemical state, a lost opportunity. It could be the payment of never receiving something we should have received, had we not transgressed.

Life may be unfair. Those who commit murder are not always caught, not always punished. But they will receive natural justice. Their minds may not be tortured, their bodies not imprisoned - but they will pay. The scales will be balanced in the end; if not in one life, then in another. The soul keeps records. Transgressions are placed in the minus column of the ledger. You will be accountable for them at some point.

– – –

1 Only those who have transgressed innocently - who had genuinely no idea that they were doing wrong and if they had known would not have done it - do not pay. Or if they do, it is only slight. As to how innocent anyone is, again I leave to moral philosophers.

2 Invariably, though, they will already have started.

7.

Syncretism & Elementalism

Something unique has occurred in Western society during the latter half of the Twentieth Century in respect to spirituality. It could not happen prior to this because the amount of knowledge (and ways of acquiring it) was not available even to the privileged few before certain technological developments came into existence. Simply put, all of us - should we so desire - can now find out about virtually any religion, faith or belief system in a matter of days, if not hours. Whether through reading, surfing the internet, watching television or simply conversing with others, we can access areas of infor-mation that simply could not be done a hundred years ago. It is only this century that education (and thus the ability to read) was given to almost all; only the latter half of this century that certain beliefs and philosophies (from the East, for example) were known about by anyone other than a small minority; only relatively recently that all this information could be stored in a way which can be accessed with little financial expenditure or effort.

The direct result of this has led to a revolution in spiritual thought. In times past, this revolution would have been considered heretical; ironically, it has and is now occurring with barely an acknowledgement. Over the last few decades, more and more people are no longer following one faith, but combining aspects of different faiths to create individual belief systems - in effect, people are creating their own faiths. The negative side of this has been the rise in extremist cults, which has been noted; the positive side is that, for the first time in the history of civilisation, an individual can combine religions, add their own personal beliefs, practice and state them in public and not be executed, persecuted or ostracized for doing so.

In a world where established religions are becoming more and more dogmatic or, paradoxically, collapsing due to an effort to incorporate widely differing viewpoints, Syncretism - the 'attempted union of principles at variance with one another'[1] - is becoming a viable alternative to many people and is growing at an incredible rate. The 'attempted union' has succeeded; the principles are no longer at variance. Not only can people follow an individual, syncretic path, they *are*. Christianity, Buddhism, Hinduism, Judaism, Paganism, Qabalism, Confucianism, Shintoism, Taoism: people are mixing and matching all these and many other faiths in incredible combinations and overlaying them with their own personal codes which (though it is highly likely) they do not know exist elsewhere. They are including these personal beliefs because they feel these beliefs are right for them, not because they have been exposed to them previously. For example, the belief system set out here holds precepts which are specifically Zoroastrian; yet I had never even heard of Zoroastrianism or its principles when I began to believe and follow those precepts.

It could be that we are witnessing the quiet birth of a new religion - a religion whose very foundation is different from any that has come previously and, indeed, may alter our whole perspective of what religion actually is. Instead of having groups of people (be they large or small) following one set of beliefs and principles, we will have a vast group of people following different, uniquely individual sets of beliefs and principles. In effect, what is being believed is essentially remaining the same; it is the *approach* to belief, the way belief is being practised and the combinations which are appearing, that is going through a radical change.

Christianity has three major branches, something in the region of thirty-five thousand recognised sects and approximately 850 million followers. Sounds a lot, doesn't it? Indeed, it is thought to be the largest of all world religions. Yet, if someone had the time and the resources, perhaps they would find that Syncretism is not so very far behind Christianity in terms of numbers[2] - and it is very possible that, a hundred years from now (though it is doubtful it will be recognized as such), Syncretism will be the major approach to religious belief.

* * *

The belief system written about in this book arose from a series of internal truths. I knew little about the multifarious religions and faiths that exist on this planet before my spiritual awakening, not much more since then - but the little that was learnt soon showed me that many of the truths held had previously been stated across a range of existing beliefs. There is some variation, but only of a minor nature. However, it appears that this particular *combination* of truths has no parallel. No faith or religion (as far as I am aware) holds this combination of tenets as their founding principles. If it had, I would have become a follower of that path. But it was the beliefs, the conviction that these were spiritual truths which were important, not the desire to find a faith to follow. I was not looking for something to believe in; I believed in something and was looking to find its precursor. There was none, so I made my own. Hence I became a Syncretist and hence, to give a name to this particular version of Syncretism, the development of 'Elementalism': a belief system formed around a connection to the Elements. The word 'elemental' means 'of the powers of nature'[3] - and it is this literal definition that is being used here, not the personification of the elements (gnomes, undines, sylphs, salamanders and sprites) which are collectively known as elementals.[4]

As to why I was drawn to the Elements; why these were felt to be the heart of the matter (as opposed to so many deities that could have appealed or been chosen), the reasons were both intuitive and measured. Part of it was that I had no roots in any other faith. If I had been directly descended from a Nordic lineage or a strong Christian link, if I had felt strongly drawn to Buddhism or Shamanism or Taoism, again I may well have followed that path. But my heritage is so mixed no one faith stands out from any other, and no existing faith called to me.

Whatever path is followed - with the exception of certain established religions which are open to all - there should be a grounding for that path. You cannot be a Druid if you are South American; you cannot be a Uitoto if you are Irish. These paths may be inspirational, they may give a sense of meaning, but they are not your paths. We need a background, a rooting - a blood or land connection. If you have neither of these, no matter how much you believe in that faith, you will never be truly part of it. You may gain much, but you lose so much more. Herne,

Odin, Diana; whatever is being worshipped should be *known* to you - and what is known is inextricably linked with who we are, which in turn is inextricably linked with our roots: our lineage, our gender, our ethnic and cultural background. Unless that deity (or deities) is present in your roots, has a presence in your essence, you are not a worshipper, but a shadow worshipper.[5]

However, this does not mean you cannot pay homage to them. Not being a Dakota Indian does not mean you cannot respect the Gods and Goddesses the Dakotas respect. One can take these Gods and Goddesses and worship them in a non-Dakotan way, as you can for any and all deities. The Powers That Be will not complain how They are addressed; the particular name we choose to give Them is not important; the specific rituals done of little consequence. It is the act of recognition and acknowledgement that They are there that matters.

If you feel a strong connection, but have no visions of a God or Goddess; if you feel a link, but do not see It in spirit-form; if there is no interrelation in the mind's eye with a Power through meditation, worship, sleeping dreams, waking dreams or any other method of trying to reach out to that Power, then simply pay homage in any way that feels right to you. Whatever you are drawn to will be there; It will respond in some way if It wishes to.

I believe in all the Gods and Goddesses, because they are all variations of the same Gods and Goddesses. To respect, acknowledge, worship one is to respect, acknowledge, worship all. Mithra is Ra is Horus is Ama-Terasu. The Sun, the Moon, the Planets, the Seasons, the Male and Female: all these things and many others have Gods and Goddesses linked to them; all these things have more than one name. And all these things are made of matter, of energy, of force.

Elements

Matter, force, energy: they are all Elemental in nature. They all contain the Elements. The sky is Air, the land is Earth, the sea is Water. Mithra is Ra is Horus is Ama-Terasu is the Sun is Fire. . . and in the end, no matter how much you can influence and alter the minds of men, you cannot change the direction of a tornado or a flood; you cannot stop a landslide starting from the shifting of the earth or a forest fire from the heat of the day.

For one who had no blood or land link; for one who felt no specific connection; for one who could not choose at random - where else could I go but to the one thing felt around us all, in us all, every moment of our lives? Where else could I go, if not to the Elements? The fact that these questions did not arise at the time of my spiritual awakening; that I immediately felt drawn to the Elements, had always felt drawn to them in fact, does not mean I accepted without later thought. Part of spiritual awareness is asking the question 'Why'.[6] It is not blind faith; it is also about attempting to understand, to find answers. . . to grow.

But it is still only part. The rest is pure feeling. After my spiritual awakening, the Elemental world - a world of sea and sky and land and light; of rock and tree, wind and storm, heat and flame, river and stream - became something fundamental in my life. The warmth of a fire, the wind on my face, the soil beneath my feet, the rain on my skin: these were no longer merely pleasurable sensations, but something far more. I feel transformed when one of the Elements touches me strongly. I sense its energy and become part of that energy. There is a joy in the standing of a rainstorm, with the thunder roaring and the lightning flaring in its radiance; a strength felt when body is laid upon the earth and the pulse of the land flows through you; a comfort of belonging when the flame warms your body; a sense of humility when the raging wind tears around you.

Elementalism is Paganistic in nature, in that it is not a monotheistic belief, but it is not, in the strictest sense, a Pagan path - for though it aligns itself with the three major Pagan Principles,[7] it does not seek empowerment through magick and has no specific rituals. Neither is it a religion. It is not about worship (as regards the modern understanding of the word in these days of dictatorial cults and blind adulation), but rather recognition: a paying of respect to those Forces more powerful than anything and everything that lives in this world. For me, those Forces are the Elements; to you, they may be something else - God(s) or Goddess(es), Spirits or Divinities. But spiritual belief is more than the acknowledgement of the existence of a higher authority. It is also the desire to follow a code which you hold as Truth.

Whichever Powers you venerate, whatever Forces you find yourself drawn to, these are heart and spirit attractions. The code, though, must be felt to be true by all aspects of the Self - for the code, the belief system, determines how we view this world and how we live this life. Truth is at the heart of any spiritual approach. The truth of what you believe, truth in yourself, truth to others. A spiritual belief does not lie; you either believe it or you do not. And any belief system (be it a major religion or an individual path) holds certain truths. These truths may vary; they may be subjective; they have certainly caused conflict, but they are truths nonetheless. Truths which, at their core, are simple in nature.

As is Elementalism.

Although this particular path is more extensive than has been presented so far (which will be addressed later), the basis of this belief system can be clearly stated. The ideas of Self and Soul; the need for resolution, balance, wholeness; the awareness of multiple lives and a helicoidal system; the enactment of transgressions and payment, beneficence and reward - essentially, that is all there is to it. Simple truths; simple faith. 'Elementalism' is not just a reference to the Elements; it is also a reference to the elementary nature of this spiritual path.

Some may dismiss this path - and many other faiths being followed - as New Age nonsense (despite the fact that a number of these faiths are very old indeed). Perhaps they are right. Perhaps the thousands who are following these paths are achieving nothing corporally. Perhaps there are no Forces, no Gods and Goddesses, no Powers That Be. Perhaps there are no patterns. Perhaps there is no purpose, no balance - that it is all just neurological stimuli, cell structures, synapses and meaningless existence. It does not matter. This New Age nonsense *works* for many who are practising it. It is more than Maslow's self-actualization theory. These faiths bring with them, along with many other things, an acceptance that what happens happens for a reason - and with that acceptance comes a sense of peace even in the darkest times; a calm within no matter how damaging the hurricane. If all these faiths are just so much New Age nonsense, then this New Age nonsense improves many people's lives - and it often improves the lives of others who interact with those people.

Is that so very wrong?

– – –

1 *Collins English Dictionary*, 1972 edition.

2   In fact, I have met a number of Christians who hold some distinctly non-Christian beliefs. So, are they Christians or are they Syncretists?

3 *Collins English Dictionary*, 1972 edition.

4   Similarly, 'elementalism' is defined as 'the belief that the gods [and goddesses] of antiquity were to be identified with the forces and aspects of nature.' (*ibid.*). However, as I consider all gods and goddesses - antique or otherwise - to be reflections of nature and the Elements, I have in effect slightly redefined the usage of the word in this book.

5   This is possibly why some people who are moving ever onwards from one faith to another find none that fits. They are looking for a path with their head alone, not their Self in its entirety. They are searching for a discipline, the way a faith is followed, rather than the reasons why a faith is being followed - the method, not the cause. It is the rituals they are attracted to, not what is being ritualized.

6   There are those who would disagree with this, who would say that the whole concept of rationalisation has adversely affected our way of believing; that we have lost our connection to the land and the old ways, forgotten ancient knowledge, precisely because of the imposed idea of Reason which was laid upon us during the age of Enlightenment. This Shamanic approach is one many of us envy. We wish we could let go of our own need to analyse, reject sometimes the logical processes our minds automatically apply to any question. But we are a product of generations of Enlightened thinkers and many of us have not yet reached a point in our spiritual

development where we can break entirely free of Reason's chains - and so, until that time comes, we have no choice but to continue asking the question 'Why'.

7 '(1) Love for and Kinship with Nature; (2) The Pagan Ethic: 'If it harms none, do what thou wilt'; (3) Honouring the totality of Divine Reality. . . without suppression of either the female or male aspect of Deity.' (The Pagan Federation: *Pagan Federation Declaration*).

II: Stepping Carefully Through the Undergrowth

"Only when we turn thoughtfully toward what has already been thought, will we be turned to use for what must still be thought."

Martin Heidegger

8.

The Four Major Forms of Interaction

Because a belief system is not only about recognition and respect of the Powers That Be, but also about how we live our lives; because a belief system lays down a moral code, a 'rule book' which we try to follow; because a belief system directs us to a certain extent in how we approach life and the choices we make during it; because a belief system gives us, in essence, a spiritual *Weltanschauung* or world view, by necessity that belief system will (or should) also determine how we interact with those we come across during our lives.

There are various kinds of interactions between people. From shop assistants to colleagues, taxi-drivers to neighbours, we make contact with many different people in many different ways. However, of these differing contacts, there are only four that play a considerable and considered part in our lives: lovers, friends, family and enemies. Colleagues may be pleasant or unpleasant to us at work, but when we move on we leave behind that interchange; it is only when they become friends or lovers that they still hold a place in our thoughts. Similarly, neighbours may be close or distant to us, but the extent of their importance arises from friendship or loathing. In regard to long-term cause and effect, action and reaction, damage and benefit, it is lovers, friends, family and enemies who play substantial roles in the lives we lead.

Therefore any belief system has to address these four major types of interaction if it is to be of use in the practical sense of day-to-day living. However, in regard to these interactions, truth can often be intertwined with desire: what we wish to be so can overwhelm what actually is. In writing about lovers, friends, family and enemies, I found myself constantly struggling to write what was intuitively felt and experientially known to be truth, as opposed to what I wished was the truth. I hope we all find someone we can love deeply who loves us just as much, for example; the truth is we do not. There are people who do not find happiness in love - and there are reasons under the belief system presented here why this occurs. They are unpleasant to state, but truth is truth; it is not concerned with pleasantries.

As to how successful I have been in unwinding what we would like to be true and what is genuinely true will have to be judged by you. If you disagree with what is being said here, you could well be right. If truth is subjective, then the truths written below may be the most subjective of all.

(i) First Loves, Lifemates, Soulmates and Partners

Potentially, we have three important lovers in our lives: our First Love, our Lifemate and our Soulmate. The first is the person we fall very much in love with; the first whose wants and needs are considered equal to our own. This is not necessarily the first love we have. When we are young, our first lover may well be someone we believe we love totally - but we realise later in life that what we thought was love then was not actually love. It was an introduction to love, not love itself. Someone may have a first love at sixteen which is a genuine First Love, but most of us do not have one until much older.

The second is the person we commit ourselves to totally. We love them in a much more rounded way than our First Love, and we know that in our heart of hearts we will never leave them. For some, of course, the heart changes and they do. For others, their Lifemate changes into someone who is no longer their Lifemate and they leave. For yet others, their Lifemate leaves them. And for still others, their Lifemate changes, the changes are liked, but the Lifemate leaves anyway.

You may be my Lifemate; it does not mean that I am yours.

The third is the person we bond to, bind to, become one with. They are part of us and we of them.[1] When they are not present, we sometimes feel as if part of us has left with them, and the rest of us feels a little confused. Yet sometimes, even though we find our Soulmate, we lose them. Even Soulmates do not always stay together; they did not earn the right to. Previous transgressions have determined this will not be.

Some people are very lucky. They find all three in one lifetime. It is a life full of joy and pain in terms of their emotions, but it is also a rich and satisfying one. Some have two of those lovers in one: the First Love becomes the Lifemate or the Lifemate becomes the Soulmate.

A very rare and lucky few have all three in one: the First Love becomes the Lifemate becomes the Soulmate. It is possible that these people are on their last life of the cycle; at least many of us would like to think this is so.

Part of our life is about finding these loves. Another part is nurturing them and being nurtured, so that one becomes another (the First Love to the Lifemate) and another still (the Lifemate to the Soulmate). A sadder part is the realisation that this is not going to happen and saying goodbye. The saddest part is losing them when you do not want to because they no longer want that continuance for reasons of their own. In between are the other, less important lovers - the might-have-beens - but something was not right.

Some people never feel this. Their lovers are a part of their lives, no more important than their work, their ambitions, their aspirations, their friendships, their spiritual development. That is right for them. But for those who hold the loving of someone above all other things (even though they may be balanced enough not to revolve their lives around the lover, due to the knowledge that this puts an immense amount of unfair responsibility and pressure on the one they love), that love becomes the most fundamental part of their life, more important than anything else.[2]

The immediate 'knowing' (or love at first sight) of our First Love, our Lifemate, our Soulmate - the Three Great Loves - happens to only very few. They are not like jaguars; they do not unexpectedly jump out on us from behind the foliage. For most of us it is a gradual process; fireflies who gently shine when we see them. The Three Great Loves are invariably people we are attracted to over time. They evolve into such by who they are and what they do. But though the Three Great Loves all enter at some point into our sphere, although we do make contact with them during our life, we can miss them.[3] Many of us never connect with all three and so are left emotionally unfulfilled. We fail to recognise what they could be. It may be that our view is obscured by other matters and we do not see the signs. More often, though, it is because we are with Partners.

Partners are those people we are fond of. They can make us happy and we them. There is love there. But a part of you knows this is not the right one; part of you is unfulfilled in the relationship you share. We all want to love and be loved; we all want to be validated. So we struggle to keep the partnership going, even though we suspect this should not be. The fear of loneliness can often outweigh the fear of lovelessness - and many of us refuse to take the chance of giving up what we have in order to possibly discover a wholer love.

This can lead to affairs with other people. It can lead to making sure there is someone waiting for you before you leave the one you are with. In the end, though - exhilarating as it may be to play these games - what it leads to is unhappiness within yourself, unhappiness for your Partner and later payment for transgressions done.

Alternatively, it will lead to disappointment and longing, perhaps bitterness and anger too. To stay with a Partner - someone who is not one of the Three Great Loves - is to resign yourself to a reality that your life could have been a happier one. It will lead to a partnership that slowly becomes colder and more mundane. It leads to two people sharing the same home, not two people living together and loving each other; co-existence, not closeness. It may be better than ending up alone, but it is not much better. Life is full of expectations unfulfilled and dreams unrealized; to have this in regard to love makes the pill bigger and more bitter. At least if you tried and failed to find your Soulmate, you know you tried - and if you constantly search, you only fail at the end of this life and so do not have much time to contemplate that failure. If nothing else, life will be more exciting in that search than it would be settling for a Partner. But this will only be a preference for some. To still be seeking at seventy than sitting with someone we have few feelings for is hardly an ideal alternative; maybe it is better for most to settle for a Partner than to risk ending up alone. So many of us do, after all. It all depends on the capacity for love you have and the placement it has in the hierarchy of your life. If that placement is high, the capacity great, a Partner will never make you happy. Only one of the Three Great Loves can do that.

(ii) Core Elementals

Just as we strive to balance the four aspects of Self within us to move towards wholeness, so we have external balancers. Just as those four internal aspects are made of the heart, head, spirit and body, so our external balancers fill these roles. One of these balancers will be our head: the person we talk and think things through with. The second is our heart: the person we turn to most when we need emotional support, the first we want to inform of personal happiness. The third is our body: the person who is solid for us and keeps us active. The fourth is our spirit: the person who gives us cold comfort and keeps us going when we just want to stop. These four are usually the closest friends we have; the friends who will do almost anything for us, will always be there for us in their own particular way. These are our 'Core Elementals' - individuals who play an Elemental role in our lives. Without them that life would be much poorer.

However, Core Elementals are not simply close friends; occasionally, they are not even close. You may be a Core

Elemental for someone, but that person may neither be one of your Core Elementals nor a close friend. You just like being in their company. Though it is rare, not all close friends are Core Elementals; not all Core Elementals are close friends. A Core Elemental may hardly ever be seen or spoken to; all that is required is that you can *potentially* see and speak with them if you need to.

The aspect we connect to with a Core Elemental is not necessarily their own base. A head-based person may not be a head-based Core Elemental with you. They are primarily an Air person, but you may access their body aspect, the Earth side. You may both talk about your experiences, bounce ideas back and forth, but the time spent with each other will mainly revolve around doing things you physically enjoy. You will not sit around talking about life and the universe. Similarly, you could be body-based, but have a friend access your head, your Air side. Though you may go out and do things together, you will be constantly talking about life and the universe, about problems and ideas. The aspect of the Self accessed does not have to be the base aspect for either Core Elemental. Though it is unusual, two spirit-based people, or a head-based person and a body-based person, may play a heart-based role with each other.

Neither is it the case that Core Elementals fill the same role with each other. Two Core Elementals may both play a heart-based role - if one is emotionally upset, they will talk to the other first and most and visa versa - but this does not have to be so. A heart-based Core Elemental for one may be a body-based Core Elemental for the other. The conversations will move from emotional subjects to practical subjects and back again at an incredible rate. Neither will ever have any difficulty in doing this.

Core Elementals are not fixed; they can and do grow apart.[4] Our lives change; we change. One of our Core Elementals may drift away because they move in a new direction that does not need our involvement. We may move away from them for the same reason. You have both played the role you needed to play in each other's lives and it is time to move on. You do not mourn the loss of a Core Elemental, because that moving away is a slow, natural leaving.

No Core Elemental moves out of your sphere before their time, unless they are trying in some (usually unknown) way to hurt you, or because you have hurt them. If it is the former, they will pay for that transgression; if it is the latter, you will pay for yours. That is why you should never abuse their friendship - not because you will lose them, but because you will hurt them deeply. No friend deserves to be that hurt, because any friend - especially a Core Elemental - is only a friend because they feel a bond with you. Break that bond for no good reason and you have transgressed.

Similarly, Core Elementals can change their roles with you and visa versa. All Core Elementals can potentially use any of your four aspects as their primary link with you and you with them. You may fill a head-based role with me, but I could change that role over time. This is not a problem. Our roles evolve and change quite smoothly; if I change my role with you, you may change the roles of your other Core Elementals - or one may leave your sphere, or you leave theirs, or a new one appears. As long as there are no transgressions made, that we do not suddenly cut a Core Elemental out of our lives, these alterations in our roles are not traumatic and we accept them happily. Furthermore, it is usually the case that when one of your Core Elementals leaves, another soon takes their place, even when they left unnaturally. As long as you do not transgress against them, you will not find yourself without one of your external balancers for any length of time. Unless you yourself do not allow it.

There is loneliness and *loneliness*. Some people, because of their lack of self-worth, refuse to make good friendships. Others do it for many other reasons - image, callousness, damage, bitterness and so on and so on. All these people are missing something special. Core Elementals fulfil a certain need in our lives; if we cannot access them because they are not there, we do not gain that fulfilment and our lives will seem somehow emptier. Even if we have someone we love with us, with a Core Elemental missing we will feel something lacking in our lives - for a Great Love is a distillation of all four aspects, not a magnification. They may be the most important thing in our lives, but they cannot possibly satisfy the need for the four external aspects. A Great Love can never take the place of the Core Elementals. No one person can do it; they do not have the capacity to be four in one and they will resent you for burdening them in that way. So if you shut out your Core Elementals and focus on that one important love exclusively (we call it obsession), you will lose.

If we have no love at all or are with someone we no longer love (or never did), to be without one or more of our Core Elementals means we will be lonely even more.

A lot of people do not have or need four Core Elementals. They are quite happy with two or three. Usually, though, one or more of these Core Elementals is filling more than one role. We can, for example, be primarily a head-based Core Elemental for someone, but if it is needed we can double up and become both head- and heart-based for them. We can even cover three roles. However, it is very difficult for a Core Elemental to take on all four aspects.

It puts a great strain on the friendship, as the Core Elemental doing this will start to feel under a lot of pressure. In practical terms, they will feel their friend is giving them no breathing space; that they are being too demanding. If the Core Elemental being used in this way is in a relationship, life becomes even more difficult. The lover may become very jealous of all the time being spent with the close friend. Good relationships can end over this sort of thing. It comes down to a 'me or them' situation and that is disastrous for all concerned.

In its simplest form, Core Elementals work in the following way:

DIAGRAM 2

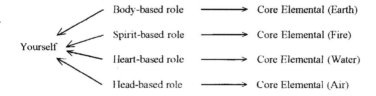

But Core Elementals may have far more convoluted connections to each other, for example:

DIAGRAM 3

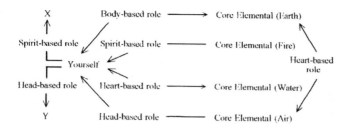

Or (in the cases of groups who are highly intertwined in respect to friendship and relationships, or who live in small communities):

DIAGRAM 4

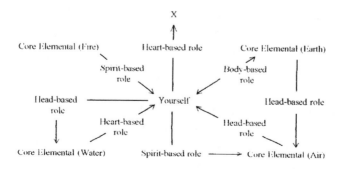

There are many variations of how Core Elementals work for and with each other; the permutations that occur can be astonishingly complex, the combinations vast in numbers - but there is one basic rule that always applies. If you are a Core Elemental to someone, they will confide in you in a way that is done with no-one else, except perhaps to another Core Elemental. One should not break that confidence. To do so is again a transgression, as it is a betrayal of trust. However, some confidences you have been told need to be thought over with another - and here careful judgement is called for. By nature we tend to form ourselves into groups. Friends of ours become friends to each other; friends of our friends become friends of ours. As such, objective opinions are difficult to find. Even your lover (if you have one) may have an agenda of their own. Therefore, when seeking an opinion from someone who is in an objective position, it is important to bear in mind that the 'objective position' may not always be as it appears.

There are two key words when it comes to being a Core Elemental: loyalty and availability. If you are a Core Elemental for someone, they have to trust you implicitly and you should always be there for them. You should do this because you too have your own Core Elementals, and you would expect both these things from them. What you expect, so should you give. Once again, it comes down to balance.

(iii) Blood Ties

The first truth about the family is that just because we are blood related does not mean we have to like each other. The second truth about the family is that this is often the case.

As the Twentieth Century has progressed, the idea(l) of the family unit has been fast collapsing, until it now only exists in 'feelgood' cinema and advertising. Virtually all societies are based on the principle of money coming into the home and money going out; as of this time of writing, only a minority can support this system singlehandedly. The rest of us, especially those in the mortgage-couple-children situation, have to do it jointly.

For Western society in particular, one person cannot stay at home and nuture while the other goes out and provides. This is no bad thing: we may have lost a stable environment for our progeny, a confusion over roles and relationships breaking down faster than the unpacking of the belongings, but there are also less unhappy, frust-rated, brutalized women, more independence and equality and greater choice in how we live our lives. As always, there is loss and gain; there is balance of a sort. The trad-itional lifestyle may have all but departed, but like most traditions, its value is in its connotations, not its practical use. To mourn the loss of something that no longer functions adequately in today's society is a pointless exercise. It is fine to preserve steam trains, but we hardly wish to use them for long-distance journeys.

It is not my intention to posit an alternative system of living, nor to suggest ways of changing the system we have. The only area being considered here is what is acceptable and unacceptable in terms of interaction with members of the family. Is it wrong, for example, to sever communication with your family if the members of that family constantly clash with you? Do blood ties mean a debt is owed? Is it a transgression to ignore those blood ties? Should any spiritual path allow you the right to reject the family?

These are questions which need not be faced in a family unit that is supportive. Families may have agreements and disagreements, show approval or disapproval, but if there are bonds there - a genuine liking or at least non-disliking between the members of the family - then the individuals in that family should be treated like all other individuals you feel connected to (albeit this is not always the case). If you believe blood ties are important, that the family should not break down no matter how much you all go your separate ways, then you will act as such. If you believe blood ties are irrelevant, that there is no need for support, then you will also act as such. But the question still remains: what is right and wrong in regards to interaction with the family.

Under the belief system laid down here, this question is answered purely through the idea of justice. No debt is owed to parents simply because they brought you into this world and nurtured you through those years when you could not survive independently. It was their choice to do so.[5] However, their beneficence may lead you to feel they should be rewarded; any transgressions made against them may result in you feeling that you should make up for those transgressions somehow; if resolution is still outstanding then resolution should be attempted. The same system of justice applies to siblings, children and other members of the family. If you feel debts are owed, resolution needed, then you should make payment, try to resolve.

What should not be expected is reward for your own beneficence. What is given - whether to family or otherwise - should be given freely. Reward may come, but it should not be covertly demanded in the giving. If reward is due, but does not materialise, then the person who fails to deliver this justifiable reward has transgressed and they will pay for it. The primary aim as always is for you not to transgress, to fail making payment. What others do or not do is their own problem. The fact that they are family makes no difference; the problem is still theirs, not yours.

(iv) Negative, Positive, Causal and Self Hatred

There are people in this world who are simply destructive. They are Cold Selves who allow that Coldness free reign. They enjoy the act of deliberately hurting and harming others. Some of these destroyers may select you as a victim, due to the colour of your skin, your sexuality, your gender, your personality or any number of other untenable reasons. If this is the case, the only option available is to keep as far out of their reach as possible, endeavour to show no reaction or response to the harm they cause you (or at least not directly; rage where they cannot hear you) - and hope they either get bored of a game with no result or that they select another Cold Self, in which case (with luck or sadness, depending on your level of empathy) they will destroy each other. This type of hatred - the act of emotionally, mentally and/or physically harming someone who has done no harm to you - I call 'Negative Hatred'.

Then there are people who set out to destroy due to an unfounded belief that they have been hurt by another. The people who desire this sort of destruction are invariably Damaged Selves. The more connected you are to this Damaged Self, the more likely you will be the object of this destruction. Friends who have wrongly perceived your actions as being hurtful or believe you were involved in hurtful actions when you were not; lovers who are no longer with you but still love you; Great Loves who you left or left you for another but still have feelings for you - if any of these are Damaged Selves, they will turn that love into a form of hatred, become vindictive and seek vengeance. It is that old adage: the more they hurt you, the more it means they care. This type of hatred - the act of emotionally, mentally and/or physically harming someone who you care about - I call 'Positive Hatred'.

Positive Hatred is irrational. To try to analyse it, to find the logic behind it, is self-defeating. It can be understood, but it can never be rationalized - because the premise on which it is based is a false one. The person who feels this hatred genuinely believes they have been hurt in some way by you, even though this is not the case;[6] indeed, it may very well have been they who initialized the damage. The guilt or shame of their own actions, the wish to deny what they have done, leads them to turn what actually occurred upside-down, so they come to believe that *they* were harmed, they were the victim, they who suffered. Honourable actions done, good intentions carried out by you are twisted into being seen as dishonourable and bad; actions never made by you are perverted into actions that should have been made, but deliberately held back; knowledge and acceptance of things that made you the individual you were are now seen as unacceptable.

The more damaged the Self, the more love they feel for you, the fiercer their desire for vengeance, the more vicious their hatred. The result will either lead to continuous attacks until the Damaged Self feels that retribution has been enacted and the hatred, the desire for vengeance dissipates - or it will lead to a series of attacks that build in their viciousness until there is one last monumental attack. The latter is the type which attracts media interest. It makes headline news, invariably with one or more deaths attached. Crimes of passion: attacks by Damaged Selves against those they love.

There are also people who set out to destroy due to a correct belief that they have been hurt by another. You did harm them, they hate you for that harm and are actively seeking vengeance for it. This type of hatred - the act of emotionally, mentally and/or physically harming someone who hurt you - I call 'Causal Hatred'.

It is causal because there is due cause for this hate to be felt. Harm was done to - or someone close to - the individual who feels this hatred. However, though in one sense Causal Hatred is understandable, in that the person who hates rightfully feels wrong has occurred and seeks vengeance for this wrong, both hate and vengeance are in themselves transgressions. To feel hate, to desire vengeance, to fantasise about committing acts of vengeance, these are part of the natural process of healing when hurt has been levelled upon you. You want justice; you want them to hurt like you do. Time and life will lessen that hate and that craving for revenge. However, to project hate, to enact vengeance, is to transgress - the more hate shown, the more vengeance meted out, the greater the transgression grows. It leads to a larger payment being made, a greater descent on the spiral.

Natural justice is not a tool for your use; you do not have the right to impart it. Natural justice has to occur in its own time and place, in its own way. Those who have hurt you will make payment. The fact that you may no longer feel hate or desire vengeance when it does occur is neither here nor there. Natural justice is not con-cerned with what you want, because it is not an entity; it is a natural force like energy or motion. It delivers payment for transgressions made when most opportune to do so. If you enforce that payment early, if you seek justice by your own hand, then you are going against a natural force. Vengeance is unnatural justice; you will suffer for it - and those who have received that vengeance may get off lightly. Your vengeance may be lesser than the one they would have received if you had let natural justice take its course.[7]

Of all hatreds, Causal Hatred is the least transgressional in its materialisation (though not necessarily in the acts that result from this hatred). For those who hate and seek vengeance for no, misconstrued or twisted reasons, their transgressions are far greater - as will be their payment.

Finally, there are people who set out to destroy themselves. This destruction can be a mixture of conscious, sub-conscious and unconscious thought. Someone who commits suicide can be working very much on a conscious level; someone else may destroy their life with no conscious recognition of what they are doing. This type of hatred - the act of emotionally, mentally and/or physically harming oneself - is known as Self Hatred.

Self Hatred manifests itself in various ways. It may be directed totally inward, or it may be directed internally *and* externally. The fact that some people deal with a lot of the hurt inflicted on them (real or imaginary) through vengeance can result in direct or indirect response. They hurt and feel the need to hurt back. If they have been physically attacked, they will attack physically; if they have received mental cruelty, they will lash out with mental cruelty - but if vengeance cannot be returned in kind, they will enact it via some other method. However, this cannot always be done to the person who originally hurt them (indeed, sometimes there is no person, for no harm was done). The consequence of this unavailability may result in redirection: innocent bystanders are harmed instead. The desire for vengeance is out of control.

Whatever the case - inflicting vengeance or failure to inflict vengeance; vengeance on the transgressor or on innocent parties - there has been a failure to deal with the pain. Revenge is not resolution; returning the pain is not removing the pain. Vengeance may allow gratification; it may lessen the pain felt by yourself, a smothering of the bitter with sweet, but it is not a letting go of the pain. It may give you an excuse not to think about the pain, to stop feeling it - but all you are doing is failing to treat that pain inside of you. Things that are not treated rot and fester, and in that rotting they affect the surrounding areas.

Some of us grow stronger from the pain dealt to us; some of us become damaged. Those who grow stronger may be more cautious, a little less trusting initially, but it does not affect how they feel about the people they meet or close them off from the world. The antibodies clear up the wound. But those who are damaged, who let the wound rot and fester, begin to destroy. They may do this by eating away at themselves through self-loathing ('I deserve this hurt'), lack of self-worth ('I do not deserve not to be hurt') and low expectation ('I will be hurt'). They create a self-fulfilling prophecy ('I will never be happy; I will always be hurt') and set about making it so. They become sad and depressed and lonely and (often) alone. But it can also work the other way round. Self Hatred can lead to ensuring that others are hurt before they can hurt you, even though they have no intention of doing so. This Self Hatred leads to destroying what you love before that love gets too deep. The rose is not seen, only the thorn - and the thorn is plucked out and discarded with the rose still attached. They hurt those who love them; push away those who care.

This kind of Self Hatred is again a hatred Damaged Selves specialise in. Part of being damaged is the unrecognized desire *to* damage. Damaging and destroying others shows the Damaged Self that they still have strength, still have power; that they are still in control. And so those who are damaged damage others and thus further hurt themselves in what they lose; feeling hurt, they then blame those whom they hurt, and so continue to damage others in an ever increasing vicious circle until there is no-one left who cares. They become bitter and angry and lonely and (invariably) alone.

This will be done through selfishness, thoughtlessness, callousness, coldness, deceit, delusion, lies, betrayal - whatever will achieve the desired result. But it will always be subtle, always manipulative. To be caught out means that *you* will know what the Damaged Self is up to; your hurt will be no less, but you can tell others what has been done. Damaged Selves do not want to be exposed; they always want to be seen as the victim. They only want their side of the story told or no story told at all. Damaged Selves are secretive and they plan far ahead. They will be aware of possible exposure, are ready to push away all who become cognisant of their transgressions. Damaged Selves dip toes in many different pools; if one looks as though it is about to dry up, they will already be swimming in another. One circle of friends will be abandoned for another group; old interests will be dropped as new interests (and attendant enthusiasts) suddenly become fascinating, or an interest is maintained which is completely separate from the rest of their lives. You may have previously been introduced to some members of this other circle, may have been allowed to skirt the outside of these interests, but you will never be permitted to fully enter.

Damaged Selves have to do this, because they are not aware they are doing it. They consider it is being done for other reasons: a desire to move on, a belief that a friendship is not working, a conviction that an old relationship is failing and a new relationship will be better for all concerned. They will be secretive and subtle and manipulative because they convince themselves that they are trying not to hurt anybody. The sadness is they cause so much greater hurt because of their covert machinations. A further sadness is that they harm themselves most of all. Their low self-esteem may be disguised by a high sense of self-importance (Damaged Selves rarely admit they are wrong, but rather backtrack to a point where they can state that what they said or did was misinterpreted and what was intended was the opposite of what was said or done), their Self Hatred may be wrapped in a blanket of eternal optimism (Damaged Selves usually believe that *this* friendship, *this* relationship will work, but that belief always fades as the new becomes old) - but in the end they throw away what they have through that Self Hatred. They just believe it was taken from them.

– – –

1 Always bearing in mind that even the perfect Soulmate is not perfect twenty-four hours a day.

2 These people are more often than not heart-based people. For heart-based people, the person you love is at the centre of your heart. However, some heart-based people have the capacity for so much love, they feel the need to love more than one person (as opposed to loving more than one person for selfish gratification), while others smother their lover in love so much, the lover feels stifled. If you are looking for love, no-one loves as deeply as a heart-based person - but that love can be damaging and dangerous.

3 As to whether there is just one Soulmate for each person in the world or many is a pointless debate. In either case, Soulmates cross each others' paths. The reality is that a Soulmate does not exist ready-formed, only the potential Soulmate. The rest is up to us. The same, of course, applies to our First Love and Lifemate too.

4 Alternately, they move closer together and become a couple. This often occurs and again does not present a real problem. Couples can be both lovers and Core Elementals for each other. The problems occur if that relationship breaks up. To have a Core Elemental who becomes a lover to no longer being a lover often results in the loss of the Core Elemental as well. You not only lose a lover but a close friend too - causing much sorrow for both of you as well as for your other Core Elementals, especially if you and your ex-lover share one or more of these Core Elementals. This is why the break-up of relationships cause such harm to some groups while hardly any to others. It all depends how interlinked that group is in terms of Core Elemental roles.

5 That choice may be very limited, of course. Accidents happen. There are fathers who never wanted to be fathers; mothers who, for various reasons, could not or were unable to have abortions and so became reluctant mothers. Often, this reluctance fades in time and is replaced by love. Sometimes, though, this does not happen - only unwilling acceptance or abdication of responsibility. There are abandoned children and children who are not loved. But the sexual act occurred, the accident happened, the child born. There was choice there, even though the consequences of that choice were undreamt of at the time.

6   There are occasions where the Damaged Self seeking vengeance is doing so because they have been hurt by you when it was never your intention to hurt. However, the hatred felt is still irrational because, even if explained to them that the hurt was unintentional, they will never accept this was the case. They have fixed in their minds that deliberate harm was levelled at them; nothing can be said or done to alter that perception.

7   This does not mean that unnatural justice cancels out natural justice. A transgression has to be paid for; if the vengeance delivered is less than the transgression made, natural justice will ensure some additional payment occurs. However, it is possible that the payment will not be as severe as it should have been, because your transgression of enacting vengeance leads to a 'deflection' of some of that payment onto yourself.

9.

The Ascent & Descent of the Spiral

The helicoidal process of the soul - the cycle of birth, death and rebirth - is not as simple as it first seems. Though we are constantly moving up and down the spiral as we err and do good, we can be moving down with one transgression while simultaneously moving up with a beneficent act. However, one does not cancel out the other.

The spiral is actually a series of spirals entwined together. It is a kind of spiritual fibre-optic cable: inside the one spiral casing, there are many strands all spiralling around one another. If you imagine the soul as information, then that information is running along all those spirals in both directions; some parts are far ahead, some far below, all are fluctuating up and down. The actions we make, the choices we take, the harm and good we do constantly shifts this information to higher and lower points. Different actions, choices, decisions affect different parts of the information and the level they are at. And the information is interrelated; certain parts check or speed up other parts.

The spiral casing itself is not a straight up and down one. At the bottom, the coils are small, for the first steps we take when we move beyond deeds done purely for ourselves raise us considerably. The further we climb, the wider the spiral becomes around the axis - until towards the top the coils of the spiral narrow again, for the last steps we take with the high spiritual awareness gained by this time leads us to few transgressions and much beneficence.

Visually, it can be represented in the following way:

Fig. 2.1. The helicoidal process of the Soul

But this is still a simplification, because the spiral is not merely one spiral. The helicoidal process is a series of spirals connected together. The top of one becomes the bottom of another. Each spiral is a level that we have attained; when we reach the top of one level, we move on to the bottom of another. As to how many levels there are is anybody's guess. There are faiths that hold three, seven, nine, eleven levels of spiritual ascent; others believe there are none, but rather simultaneous lives - that we have an infinite number of Selves on an infinite number of worlds. There are belief systems which state there are further levels in their equivalent of the Otherworld; that when we finish the cycle of multiple lives on this world, we start again on a higher plane. Perhaps there is a point in spiritual development where the answer to this question is forthcoming (if there is one); perhaps then we learn what each level signifies regarding the ascent of our soul. If that is so, then the answer will come when we are ready to receive it. However, maybe this type of classification is unnecessary. There are as many levels as are needed; the number is not important.

Therefore, the actual spiral of spiritual growth appears thus:

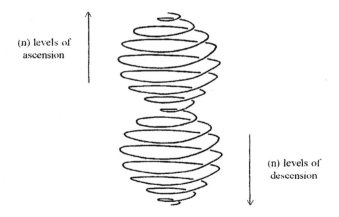

Fig. 2.2. The helicoidal process of the Soul

The points where the spirals connect - the 'crossover' or minima points - are crucial in terms of spiritual development. They are like ledges jutting out from a cliff face; we can stand on them and get some sense of overview of the surrounding terrain. But they are also testing stages. What we do following the reaching of that point will result in whether we are allowed to continue on the new level or drop back to the old and try again. If we pass the test, these crossover points become sealed to a certain extent. If we slip up, transgress greatly on the next level, our descent down the spiral is halted by these minima. The passage to the level below is blocked and we do not slide further. But this blockage is not solid; it can be broken through. There are certain transgressions so major, the descent down the spiral occurs with such force and speed that the soul 'smashes' its way through a minima seal.

As to the nature of these crossover points, these testing stages, there are two which are immediately apparent. One of them is wealth; the other is spiritual awakening.

No matter which political and economic system each person lives under; no matter how rich one person in one nation is compared to one in another, there are always people who are wealthy relative to those around them. The test, in terms of the soul's development, is what is done with this wealth. This is not simply a case of giving away money to charity or supporting noble causes; it is more how the wealth possessed (whether it be monetary or otherwise) is used in terms of negative verses positive effect. One can invest in tropical woods or tree farming, for example. Both can result in personal financial gain, job creation and attendant benefits for others - but one contributes to rainforest destruction while the other does not. On a different scale, one can buy a masterpiece by a dead artist or any number of works by living ones. Both result in aesthetic pleasure and investment potential, but the latter supports artistic endeavour far more than the former. On a different scale again, a farmer can have a surfeit of wheat from this year's crop; that excess wheat can be given to those in need of food, it can be sold for a small (or no) profit - or it can be stored to waste away or be destroyed.

Wealth brings with it large responsibility and multifarious problems. Perhaps it is the case that 'we should all have those problems,' but some of those problems we can be thankful not to have faced in this life. The test of wealth in regard to spiritual development holds within it enormous potential for failure.

The test of spiritual awakening is much simpler. Once you become consciously aware that there is more to life than simply passing through it; once you have a positive belief system (no matter whether it is an individual or established path), you either try your best to follow that system or break it when it conflicts with personal desire. The more you follow the code, the higher you climb the new level; the more you break it, the more you descend. At the end of the life in which spiritual awakening first occurred, you will either have passed or failed. The next life will find you placed on the appropriate level.

Some who follow an individual path try to get around this problem by changing their code when it suits them. They suddenly 'discover' an amendment, are given new information by the Powers That Be or become enlightened over a tenet that shows it was a false one. Occasionally, this is genuinely the case - we do get things wrong - but it is doubtful that this ever coincides with a personal desire of wishing that a tenet was not so. Elementalism holds as part of its code the idea of monogamy;[1] to suddenly become aware that polygamy was acceptable at a time when I wanted a sexual relationship with more than one person would be a highly dubious act on my part - and one that would result in greater payment for my transgression than would otherwise have occurred. Many of us may be following a path of our own development, but this does not mean we can change the direction of that path when we feel like it.

This is not to say that a spiritual path should not include the flexibility to adapt. Part of the attraction of certain faiths (especially Pagan ones) is that they happily allow this to occur. Druidry survived the onslaught of Christianity precisely because of this. The rejection by many people of several established religions has partly been due to those religions refusing to adapt and develop. How can one unquestioningly support the Roman Catholic faith, for example, when it refuses to accept birth control at a time when overpopulation in certain areas is causing so much misery and suffering. Purism - the refusal to adapt or change whatever the circumstances - should be left to retired army colonels and those who can afford to live in the past.

However, there is adaptability and change and there is hypocrisy. Returning to the example of monogamy, it would be one thing if the Pope stated that birth control was acceptable, quite another to state that polygamy was no longer a sin. There is a need for one and not for the other. If 99% of the male population suddenly became infertile or died, then there would be a need for the Roman Catholic faith to alter its stance on polygamy.

To become spiritually aware in a lifetime and to successfully pass that testing point means you will be given the opportunity to repeat that awakening in the following one. As each subsequent life is lived, the earlier the awakening and the more life given to follow a spiritual path, to attempt to balance, to resolve and not transgress. It is *the* seminal point in spiritual development - for without it, one is travelling without a map and no knowledge of your destination. There are minima points above it, but none so essential to the ascendancy of the soul. As to these other minima testing points, various theories and suggestions could be posited and put forward, but they would be just that - theories and suggestions. It is only the two above which are readily apparent.

To become spiritually aware allows you to view the events that have previously occurred in your life and the choices you made in a far more balanced way. You stand on the ledge and you get that overview; you see the reasons why what happened happened. You realise that what seemed unfair before was in fact natural justice; that what was considered luck was actually reward. The patterns emerge and you note which of those patterns need alteration and which should be allowed to continue. Those patterns which need totally redesigning you redesign. But spiritual awareness gives you more than this. It also allows you to view certain events in hindsight *as they actually occur*. It extends the possibility of seeing the effect of choices before you make those choices, to view the results of an alternative before you take that alternative. In the forest of life, it helps you to step more *carefully* through the undergrowth. It heightens your level of caution before making decisions which could lead to personal transgression - and it helps you to accept that the pain you suffer in life, each blow you take, happens for a reason. You may not always know what that reason is (some payments were started in previous lives and have yet to be finished), but there are reasons nonetheless.

Mentioned earlier in this chapter was the possibility of breaking through a minima seal through certain transgressions; transgressions so great the resultant descent on the spiral is one in which you 'smash' your way through that seal. To deliberately choose to do this - to purposely decide on a transgressional action when spiritually aware this could occur seems, to put it mildly, unwise to the extreme. Yet not only is it done, it can be done by souls who have ascended to a high level on the spiral. When it comes to self-gratification, it seems that the wise can be jut as foolish as the rest of us.

– – –

1 See Chapter 12

10.

Cardinal Transgressions; Cardinal Benefactions

Transgressions and beneficence can be broken into three main categories: minor, major and cardinal. What goes where in the first two categories depends very much on personal belief, but even here there is rough approximation. What is placed highly on the 'list' of major transgressions by one faith may appear lower on another, but there is general agreement that this act of transgression is a serious one. Similarly, the hierarchy of benefactory acts may differ in their placement with one another in respect to the particular spiritual path being followed, but none consider (all other things being equal) the returning of a lost coat to its owner as being on a corresponding level to someone donating their life savings to famine relief. From an Atheist to a Zoroastrian, most of us basically concur on the groupings of transgressional and benefactory acts.

However, whereas there may be much ethical deliberation as to hierarchical placement in respect to minor and major transgressions and benefactions, cardinal transgressions and benefactions are not subject to great debate. These acts of such high or low standing are so far removed from other acts that it is the moral equivalent of a whaleshark and a guppy: they may both be fish, but there the commonality ends.

The paradox is that not all of these acts are obvious at first. There are some cardinal transgressions and benefactions which may not readily be apparent. The reason for this is that transgression and beneficence are not applicable in the same way as principles and tenets. They are not a general code of conduct, but specific acts which differ with each particular set of circumstances. The result is that, though there may be cardinal acts of transgression and benefaction, there are no cardinal *rules*. Cardinal transgressions and benefactions are not inflexible in the same way as, say, the Ten Commandments. Loyalty is considered to be a virtue, for example - but loyalty can be a transgression *and* a beneficent act, depending on what one is being loyal to. Loyalty to a friend is generally good practice, but (to use an extreme example) if that friend is a psychopathic killer who has not been caught, then refusing to expose them out of loyalty is a transgression. Furthermore, transgressions and benefactions affect others to different degrees. The fact that a cardinal transgression results in no great harm to one person does not mean it is not a cardinal transgression, and this is equally true of beneficence. A cardinal act is defined as cardinal in respect to the *intention* of the act, not the result of that act. Under natural justice, to attempt and fail to murder is as cardinal a transgression as to succeed.

The intention to murder for whatever motive is an obvious cardinal transgression, as is rape and sexual and/or violent abuse. These cardinal transgressions are joined by the less apparent ones of permanent physical and/or mental injury to another through physical attack or otherwise, active encouragement of large-scale damage to the environment for any reason and the deliberate destruction of two people's love for each other. Similarly, cardinal benefactions such as loss of life or permanent/serious temporary harm whilst endeavouring to save a life, with the awareness that this could result (life-sacrifice); great personal sacrifice made voluntarily in order to benefit others (self-sacrifice) and the refusal to allow harm to occur to another which may result in death or permanent/serious temporary harm to oneself (protection) are all clear cardinal benefactions, but the voluntary release of someone truly loved who loves another (love-sacrifice), loss of life or physical and/or mental suffering due to belief in a faith (martyrdom) or a humanitarian cause (persecution) may not immediately come to mind.

Times change. We may forget, depending on when and where we live, the importance of some of these cardinal acts due to a lack of exposure concerning them. Martyrdom, for example, is not a common occurrence in many countries at present. People are no longer being killed or tortured every day for their religious beliefs in many societies, so those societies have lost to some extent the relevance of martyrdom as a cardinal act. But the fundamental truth of cardinal acts will be as true tomorrow as they are today as they were yesterday. Martyrdom occurs in fewer societies and perhaps less frequently at present than it did in the past, but the act of martyrdom is still as great a sacrifice by an individual as it ever was. Cardinal acts are timeless: a great transgression is a great transgression, great beneficence is great beneficence, no matter when they occurred. To accept that someone you love loves another and to say to them 'be with that other' breaks the heart and is a supreme act of sacrifice, but no less or more so this century than it was many centuries ago. To destroy the environment has always been a great transgression; the fact that it is at the forefront of current concern does not make it a contemporary wrong, simply one that is more widely recognised. The historical dominance of Judëo-Christian religions in Western society for so many centuries - religions which did not place the protection of the environment highly in their creeds - led to a 'forgetting' of this cardinal transgression, not a non-existence of it. Before this Judëo-Christian influence, Pagan faiths considered respect for the environment as being central to their spiritual code, just as many non-Western faiths have always done.

To become spiritually aware is to know these truths. They may be worded differently depending on the path followed, they may not be worded at all, but they are present. Yet - possibly because the cardinality of these acts have been forgotten due to the changing nature of values which exist at present in a society in a state of constant flux or for reasons of personal gain or satis-faction - even those who are spiritually aware enact cardinal transgressions sometimes. Desire leads them to destroy two people's love for one another; greed leads them to damage the environment; the need for vengeance leads them to murder.

It is on these occasions - this conscious or semi-conscious decision to enact a cardinal transgression knowing it is such - that the soul of the spiritually aware individual descends the spiral at such a rate it 'smashes' its way through the minima seal. It on these occasions that this soul will not be granted in the next life they live the important spiritual crossover point they had achieved in this or a previous life. If, for example, spiritual aware-ness was the last testing stage they passed, then the cardinal transgression they make will result in the loss of that awareness being given automatically at some point in their next life. They will have to once again go through the painful process of finding it unaided. In effect, cardinal transgressions 'add' extra lives to our cycle of birth, death and rebirth - just as cardinal benefactions indirectly lead to less lives being lived, for they raise us considerably on the spiral, and the higher up the spiral we are, the less far we have to go to reach the apex.

Sometimes, even for those who are high on the spiritual spiral, the desire for something in this life outweighs the desire to step off the cycle of birth and rebirth. Spiritual awareness does not necessarily make you a better person; the holding of power or gaining of knowledge does not mean it will be used wisely. Sometimes, what is wanted *now* becomes stronger than the higher aim. The more Cold or Damaged the Self the more likely this could occur, because the ultimate aim - even for those with old souls and much wisdom and understanding - seems so far away. Which is why we should never forget the ultimate purpose to all the lives we live and why the belief in a 'better place' must always be held at the core of spiritual development.

11.

The Belief in a Better Place

The assumption behind every religion and faith that believes in life after death is that there is a place or state of being we can reach - be it Heaven, Nirvana or any of the descriptive names a faith gives it - and that this place is a better one than the world we are presently in. Some religions believe you get one life to achieve this; others believe in many lives. But all believe we can reach that state and be granted a permanent place there.

The questions which arise from this assumption - the questions of why this place or state is so sought-after; why it is felt that none of us wish to return to this world; why it is believed the Otherworld is a better one than this one - are questions that have answers which are not answers.

Life in this world is neither good or bad; it is how we see our lives in it. If someone lives a happy life, full of love and pleasure, then they are not going to consider their time on this world as a bad time. Yet if they hold a religious belief, if they have a faith, they too hope that (eventually) they will be allowed to remain in wherever they believe they go to when they die. For this is what it comes down to: death. Even the happiest life ends; even the happiest life contains the pain of losing loved ones who die - and all of us would like to see our loved ones again. We miss those who have moved on.

As for those of us who do not live blissfully happy lives; those of us who are constantly being tested, constantly having to make choices and decisions, constantly transgressing and paying for those transgressions - perhaps all of us want to stop and just *be*. Even with the awareness that the pain we feel gives us a benchmark which allows us to recognise the feeling of joy, that the joy felt can be even more joyous because we have known pain, we would rather not feel pain anymore. We want calm, peace, wholeness. Rollercoasters are thrilling, but we do not want to ride them all the time.

The life beyond this life promises the calm, peace and wholeness which we strive for in this world, but can only achieve temporarily (for even long-term achievement is not permanent achievement). The Otherworld is where we want to be because there we will know who we are completely. We remember once again all of our lives; we learn how far we have come, how far we have to go. We are no longer in doubt; we are cognisant of all the details, can see all the patterns. Reprimands may be due, but once delivered, we have the ability to see and be so much more than in this life. Whilst we are There there are *no limits*. If there is an Underworld, we may be placed in that Underworld for transgressions made in this world, but we are also placed in Overworld for the benefactory acts that we did. Time and space are no longer boundaries; we can be in all places in a state of no-time because we are not body or heart or head or spirit. The body we have, if we have a body, is not corporal; the heart, the head, the

106

spirit no longer influenced by Self, because there is no Self. There is only Soul. The Otherworld or whatever you wish to call it may not be a Paradise, but it is still better than this world because, at the very least, *we* are better while in it.

Those who have glimpsed the Otherworld, those who travel between the two in sleep and waking dreams, know this. They are not Soul while there, because they are still here - but they meet those who are. Furthermore, many see and hear those who visit this world from that world. Those on the Otherworld do indeed walk among us. Family, friends, lovers: those who have died appear and speak to those who have not. Too many have seen and heard the dead for this not to be true; far too many for them all to be deluding themselves or forming phantoms from their heart. One person who sees the unexplainable can be dismissed; one thousand cannot - and there have been many thousands who have stated this over the years. This world is linked to the next; the physical and the spiritual are connected through us. The sound made in one echoes in the other; it is just that, for many who hear on this world, that sound is funnelled, distorted - whilst on the Otherworld, all sound is clear.

As for those who have not seen the Otherworld, many believe it is there and hope they will attain their place in it. Those who do not believe in anything at all - that when we die we die, *fini* - all that can be hoped for is that their personal code leads them to live good lives and that, in turn, they will get a pleasant surprise.

Elementalism - like many faiths - holds that when we die, we do enter another world; that we will be allowed to visit this world in spirit-form while in that world; that we will be with those we have loved in this world again. It holds that we will not be allowed to stay in the Otherworld if we have not yet reached the top of the spiral, but reborn in this world (unless this world is destroyed, in which case we will be reborn in another physical place). It holds that when the spiritual apex is reached, we no longer have to be reborn in this world. None of this can be proved. The Otherworld does not have an address we can write to for confirmation and no logical arguments will ever conclusively show its existence. But ontological, cosmological, teleological arguments are not fundamentally needed for spiritual conviction. Part of the soul's progress is the holding of a belief as well as how we live the lives we live. To have a belief is to know without empirical knowledge, just as we know that each snowflake is unique without having to examine every one.

Heaven, Nirvana, place or state or world, they are all interchangeable. Perhaps we all go to where we believe we will go. Heaven is or is 'next to' Nirvana; Nirvana is or is 'next to' Valhalla. The important part of this aspect of faith is not the name or description or personal representation; it is the belief that it is there and the wish to be there. It is this belief and this wish that is part of the reason why those who have a faith strive to live as good a life as they can. To live a good life moves us closer to that place; to live a good life often makes us feel good. It truly is a case of wanting the best of both worlds.

12.

The Six Directives

Every faith places certain principles as being fundamental to the practice of that faith. The Five Pillars of Islam, the Celtic code; these are all specific principles which must be followed. To not uphold these principles means you are not a Muslim or Celt, but merely of Islamic or Celtic background. To be a practising Muslim you must make a confession of faith, pray, fast, give alms and make pilgrimage; to be a practising Celt, you must try to be loyal, honourable and hospitable at all times. If this is not done - if you are deliberately disloyal, dishonourable, inhospitable on occasions - you are not a true Celt, no matter how much you insist otherwise.[1]

Principles, tenets - the ethical code of behaviour a faith holds as part of its doctrine - can be hard to follow. Though some faiths do allow a certain amount of leniency concerning their principles (for example, the fourth and fifth pillars of Islam - Almsgiving and Pilgrimage - have 'opt out' clauses for those unable to uphold them through financial or physical impossibility), others do not. A Celt can always be loyal, honourable and hospitable, no matter what their circumstances for loyalty and honour are mental practices and hospitality at its minimum only directs that you should not turn someone away from your door (to not feed or interact due to poverty or disability is not a breaking of the principle). Thus to be a Celt often means personal desire must be subjugated. You cannot speak ill of a friend to another, no matter what wrongs they have done; you cannot be treacherous, deceptive or unfaithful; you cannot just be 'on your way out' if someone comes to visit.[2]

Because the spiritual path set out here has no absolute rules, it follows that it has no explicit principles. The belief in transgression and beneficence allows for the possibility of exceptional circumstances, even in regard to cardinal acts (the taking of someone's life to prevent that person killing many is a possible example). However, these exceptions *are* exceptional; their occurrence is extremely rare - so though Elementalism has no specific ethical code, it does contain a set of *directives*. There are practices placed highly within it; it is just that these practices are approaches we 'should try' to follow, not 'must' follow - expectational rather than ecumenical - as they allow for exceptional conditions.

The first of these directives is Truth: truth to oneself, to one's beliefs - and truth to others. To lie, deceive, delude, tell half-truths is to break the practice of Truth. Truth should be told in full at the appropriate time[3] or when requested. If you do not wish to reveal the truth - usually due to pain it may cause to yourself and/or others - then remain silent or plead a version of the Fifth Amendment: state you do not wish to speak. It is impossible for anyone to 'force' the truth out of you; part of you - no matter what pressures are being brought to bear- has to decide to state it. Fortunately, as most of us will never encounter an occasion where we are physically tortured to reveal the truth, to do this is relatively easy, though it may not always seem so at the time. It may anger others, cause you to be seen as rigid or worse (as the insistence on truth may do also), but just as we should be truthful to others rather than not, just as being true to ourselves does not include being false to others, so it is better to be true to yourself than to be false to yourself by being truthful to others. As long as no falsehood (or 'not-truth', as perhaps it should be called - for it is possible to walk between the line of truth and falsehood) is told, no transgression has been made; the directive has not been ignored.

The reason why the telling of Truth should be done. None of us like to be lied to; none of us like to be deceived or deluded; none of us like to be misdirected. It is better to hurt through truth than to delay hurt through not-truth, for in that delay the truth may hurt more. Only when it is absolutely guaranteed (and there is never an absolute guarantee; even those near death can recover) that someone will not discover a hurtful truth can a not-truth be told - for most of us would rather know where we stand than to be unsure or misled as to where we stand.[4] As we would wish, so should we do.

Some truths, as has been stated frequently previously, are subjective. However, the stating of a subjective truth is not. To be asked or decide to tell the truth as you perceive it means that you should tell that truth totally and at one time if you so feel it. It is an either/or situation: there is no grey area. To reveal only part truth or to reveal full truth over a deliberately staggered period of time so that it is disconnected - resulting in the recipient of that truth failing to recognise the truth being told - is as much a breaking of the practice of Truth as to lie or deceive. The teller of this disjointed truth may be able to say to themselves 'I have told everything', but in the way of telling, the truth has not been told, and both deception and self-delusion have occurred.

The directive of Truth leads to the problem of the 'white lie' - a lie that is told which harms no-one but benefits someone. The telling of white lies is a frequent occurrence and one which causes no concern for many people, even those who rightfully consider themselves to be very honest. It is part of everyday life. Often, it is also a clash between self-truth and the telling of truth. The need for peace and solitude can sometimes be overwhelming, for example; if we have been invited to a party the party will still go ahead without us - yet to say to the host we do not feel like attending can be hurtful or taken as an insult. So we lie and give an excuse of some sort.

They key to this problem is that a white lie should harm no-one. If no-one is genuinely harmed by the telling of a not-truth and it does genuinely benefit someone in its telling, then perhaps it should be told. It all depends on how much one feels the directive of Truth should be followed - but to follow it too literally would be to deny exaggeration and thus much humour, deny fiction and thus much entertainment. The telling of stories and joke are pleasurable; belief in Truth should obviously not wipe out that pleasure. The directive of Truth should be followed when it matters, when the living of people's lives will be affected by it.

Truth to oneself; Truth to others - it is the most important of all actions, the base of the pyramid. From it comes all other codes of conduct. Honour, loyalty, courage, discipline; the list is as long as each of us feel it to be. If one is not particular brave, it goes against self-truth to be brave; if one does not feel loyalty, one should not pretend to be loyal. To avoid transgression, we should all be aware of what we truly are - for in that awareness, we neither delude ourselves or others. We do not place ourselves on the trapdoor and so do not fall through when it opens. From Truth we see our faults; from Truth we know our qualities; from Truth we realise and then actualise. We have to look in, know ourselves, keep what we like, change what we do not - but we can only do that if we face the truth about ourselves. If we self-deceive, self-delude, refuse to acknowledge what we are (the bad as well as the good) we will deceive and delude others. If we paint a false picture of ourselves, the viewers of that picture will not truly know or appreciate the artist. We are not who we are, so will not be who we can be. We are failing ourselves - and we will fail others.

The second tier of directives, the middle level of this inverse pyramid, are those of Loyalty and Honour. After Truth, Loyalty and Honour are paramount. To be loyal to friends, family, organisations; to anyone or anything you feel connected to or affiliate yourself with - the fundamentality of this cannot be underestimated. Part of who we are is who we are joined to. Loyalty is not just verbal defence; it is also active encouragement. It is about believing in someone or something and acting on those beliefs. It is about supporting the actions of others you feel loyal to.

However, some actions by those we feel loyalty towards may be very harmful to others. It is in these cases that loyalty and ethics clash. To stand by and let them hurt another for selfish reasons, to watch as they break a code you (and/or, more importantly, they) believe should not be broken, to make an act you perceive as being a trans-gression, these are difficult things to do. Your choices are limited: you can abstain, become neutral; you can advise against the action being made and state your reasons why; you can break the bond between you, no longer associate with that you once felt loyal to. These are individual decisions which depend on individual conscience. All that is being noted here is that loyalty has limitations. To be loyal to someone who is disloyal, dishonourable even, can be done. If you feel loyalty towards them you should be loyal, as it is how you feel that matters. However, there is a difference between loyal feelings and loyal actions, and those who do not act honourably or are not loyal themselves should not receive loyal actions. To be loyal does not mean that you should always actively support; if it is the case that the recipient of your loyalty is not deserving of loyalty, to say nothing against them is enough. To support them in what you see as wrongful actions is a transgression on your own part, because Loyalty has another facet - namely, loyalty to yourself, to your beliefs. Otherwise known as Honour.

Honour - the upholding of what one believes is right in thought and deed, the enaction of stated intent in the form of promises or word given - is the exterior reflection of the Self. The Self is who we are; Honour is how we act because of who we are. The wholer, more balanced, the Warmer the Self, the more honourable our actions and outlook, the more we keep our word; the less whole, less balanced, the Colder or more Damaged our Self, the more dishonourable our actions and outlook, the more we break our word. Selfish, thoughtless, callous voicing of thoughts; hurtful, harmful, damaging actions: these are the result of dishonourable motives, which in turn are the result of inharmonious Selves.

Honour sets our parameters; Honour moulds our choices. The level of Honour we have affects how wise and beneficial those choices are. To be self-beneficial is totally acceptable; to be self-beneficial through (or resulting in) the harming of others is not. Honour is the Plimsoll line; it either keeps us safely above the water or we sink to dangerous levels. To be honourable means we do not

114

always return in kind, we do not act dishonourably when transgressions are made against us. We stay true to what we believe is right.

As to what we believe is right, again it is individual belief. A dishonourable person may make a dishonourable action and believe it is right thing to do. Natural justice deals with this; the only questions we should ask ourselves are (1) do we want to do this for ourselves more than anything else and (2) will we hurt anyone in the doing of this. If the answer is yes to both questions, it may still be the right thing to do - but not often. And when it is the right thing to do, we must be careful to minimise the hurt to others. To leave someone who loves you may be necessary; to be thoughtless, selfish, uncaring, delusional, deceiving while doing so is not - and even the Coldest, most Damaged of Selves knows when they are deceiving if nothing else. Dishonourable people may not worry about Honour, but dishonourable people do lose in the end. They pay for their actions. For those who do have honour, who do feel guilt when they act dis-honourably, part of their payment is their reflection. To look into the mirror and see pain in our eyes occurs throughout our lives, but to look into that mirror and see shame is something we ourselves allow.

The third tier of directives arises from the second. Monogamy (which is particularly associated with Loyalty), Tolerance (which is particularly associated with Honour) and a third directive that arises from the two, which I have termed *Altruity*.

Altruity does not appear in the dictionary. The reason for this is that there is no existing word for what is being expressed here. It is a combination of 'altruism' and 'generosity', for Altruity is the act of being generous in one's time and efforts for others. It does not mean that one should necessarily be generous in respect of gifts or financial donations, nor does it mean one should always put others' interests before one's own. It is simply the idea that, when in a position to do so, one should help others. That help may appear in many forms; it can be through donations or gifts, physical aid or mental support, sacrifice or compromise. It is done in the way we feel we can do. To be financially wealthy may lead to donations; to be poor, this may not be possible. If we are healthy, we can physically aid others; if we are sick, we cannot. But, no matter what our circumstances, we can all help others in their time of trouble even if it is just listening to someone who needs to talk.

Altruity arises from Loyalty, in that much of what we do for others is done for friends and family; it arises from Honour, in that part of Honour is to not refuse aid to those who are deserving of aid. It is much like magnanimity, except that altruity does not always put the needs of man first and neither does the soul have to be in a state of loftiness. Altruity places all things on an equal level; the flower is as important as the tiger, the mountain as important as the man - and when the need of one is greater than the need of another, altruity supports the greater need if equal support is not possible.

For example, sad to say, it places the non-destruction of rainforest above the need for the cutters of trees to earn a living. Rainforest destruction is leading inexorably to suffering for many; the loss of livelihood leads to suffering for a smaller number. Altruity does not put the benefit of the many above the benefit of the few - it desires benefit for all - but if that benefit is not forthcoming, the benefit of the many does come before the benefit of the few. Furthermore, a bad soul can perform acts of altruity. One can be the most, selfish, thoughtless, destructive person in existence and still help others if one so desires. Even the most hateful of people - the psychopaths, the mass-murderers, the rapists - have friends they will help. They may do it for the most perverted of reasons, the motive may not be one of altruity, but the result is the same. An act of altruity has occurred.[5]

Altruity is a directive that can be followed in many ways. An obvious one is altruity to those we care for most - namely parents, children, family, friends. . . and those we love as lovers. Of all the people we should be generous to in terms of time and effort (and indeed gifts), perhaps this person is the most deserving recipient.[6]

The path followed here is a romantic one. Elements are primal forces; they are at their most powerful in a pure state at full blast. To diffuse them is to weaken them. The same can be said for love. Because love involves all four aspects of the Self - emotion and empathy for the heart; validation and verbal communication for the head; understanding and intuition for the spirit; the sexual act and comforting touch for the body - the act of loving in Elemental terms should be a primal act. No diffusion, no half-commitment, no wavering. To quote Walt Whitman: 'When I give I give myself'.[7] That giving should be total. The fierce passion may fade as time moves by, but if love is felt a gentle passion will remain.

It is for this reason that Elementalism holds as one of its directives the concept of Monogamy. You cannot give yourself totally to more than one person simultaneously.[8] What you give may be more than enough; you may feel you have love to spare - but this does not allow you licence to spread that love around. Sexual relationships can range from casual to deeply committed, one night to a lifetime. Whatever, the directive of Monogamy means that each relationship carries with it an unwritten rule: that for the period of time the relationship exists, you are connected to that person alone. What that person does is another matter; they may have a different code or no code. The point here is that *you* do not transgress, you do not hurt - that you stay true to the code you believe in. Elementalism holds as truth that monogamy is a virtuous act; any other belief system followed which holds the same should be kept to, no matter how much your personal desire to break it. If you feel more for someone else than for the one you are with, then admit that truth and leave. Varying degrees of pain will ensue, but at least you have acted honestly and honourably. What is not permitted is a 'dual link': a time of sharing yourself between old and new. This leads to deception and betrayal - two transgressions that are high on the 'Do Not Do' (or rather 'Try Not To Do') list.

Because there should be no dual link, any new relationship can only be at a potential stage when the old is ended. If one wishes to avoid transgressing, nothing can consciously be done. To say to one person, "I will be with you," while still with another is a betrayal; physical intimacy even more so. The only option available is to state, "I want to be with you," after the old has been ended. If that offer is rejected, then so be it. To desire a new relationship must *de facto* mean the existing relationship is no longer wanted or is failing. If that is the case, you have a choice between attempting to save it through revitalisation or ending it and walking away alone. To keep that existing relationship as a back-up while searching for another is again a major transgression.

The reality, of course, is that this is hard to achieve. It is hard to keep to this directive. We are human and most of us do not want to be lonely or alone, do not want to risk giving up what we have for what we might not get. We want assurances, confirmation. Love and sex are prime motives for us - to be without either is to lack. We want space within a relationship, not space without. Principles often conflict with desire and most of us do override our principles with desire at times, especially over matters such as love and relationships. So we will fail, we will transgress. But when this is the case, it is *how* we fail that matters - whether we transgress honestly or deceitfully. The directive of Truth: you are either honest or you lie, deceive, delude. The truth wounds more initially, but in the long term it is lies and deception that cause the greater pain and damage. To lose someone you love hurts; to lose someone you love and learn they were deceiving you hurts far more. Dual links are a transgression, but not so much as dual links combined with dishonesty.

Monogamy is not the only unwritten rule relationships have. The fact is that, though you may love totally the person you are with as a lover, you may not like certain aspects of their personality. They may have a tendency towards greed or selfishness; they may be tactless or thoughtless on occasions. They may have any number of a variety of vices (as do you) - but when you love someone, you accept these less pleasant aspects of their nature. Some you may subtly (or not so subtly!) try to change; others are better left alone. Whichever, we accept to a certain degree the vices of those we love. We are *tolerant* of them.

This century has seen radical change in how we all relate to each other. Women have achieved a considerable number of rights in a considerable number of societies; ethnic groups have strived for and gained much in respect to how they are treated by those who once considered themselves superior simply because of their pale pigmentation; those who are physically and/or mentally disabled have managed some success in procuring recognition that they are equally valid as human beings; the aged are gaining a stronger voice in many countries; religions are co-existing together with less antagonism. Equality is a long way off for both women and black races; equality is an even longer way off for women who are black and black people who are considered inferior by other black people; equality may be even further away for those who are perceived as being less able because of physical and/or mental limitations through birth, accident, illness or age; equality may never be forth-coming in respect to how religious groupings view each other. We all have a long way to go before we accept each other and validate each other as we should be accepted and validated.

The directive of Tolerance is a directive that categorically states we should try. None of us would like to be judged as being of somehow less worth due to how we look or are afflicted, because of our age or our religion. There are no reasons (because there are no reasonable reasons) why a person should not be granted equality because of their sex, the colour of their skin, the physical and/or mental difficulties they have to face or the faith they believe in. One person may not be equal to another; the genius may be superior to the idiot - but both should be treated equally in terms of their humanity. One should not be treated with less regard.

We may be affected as to who we are through our experiences; part of us may be what we are through our past. Our sex and skin coloration, our physical and mental condition, our religious beliefs may result in a view of the world that has been greatly determined because of how we were and are treated due to our sex and skin coloration, our physical and mental condition, our religious beliefs. But how we approach the world and interact within it is determined by how we *wish* to do it.

Not all victims of sexual inequality hate the opposite sex; not all non-whites hate those who are white; not all those classified as physically and/or mentally disabled hate those not so classified; not all the elderly hate the young; not all believers hate the non-believers.

The Elements do not always dominate; often they are subdued. This does not mean they are less respected, that a wary eye is no longer kept on them. So if the Elements - the prime forces on this planet, far more powerful in potentiality than any existing body of people - are treated with respect, why not anyone or anything who also has potentiality. Mahatma Gandhi, Marie Curie, Mary Cassatt, Charles Drew, Franklin D. Roosevelt, Martin Luther King Jr., Susan B. Anthony, Artemisia Gentileschi, Mary Seacole, Frida Kahlo, Edward Jenner, Nelson Mandela, Stephen Hawkins, Malangatana Ngwenya, Vincent Van Gogh. All achieved great change or great things; all considered less than equal by some or many at times or throughout their lives. What we are externally counts for very little. Tolerance remembers this. The ugly can produce beauty; the beautiful ugliness. The powerful, the knowledgeable can possess little understanding or wisdom; those considered insane can be brilliant.

And the reasonable can be unreasoning. Tolerance is not just about accepting people for who they are, it is also about accepting what people believe - as long as that belief *is not extreme*. The directive of Tolerance is tolerant of everything except intolerance. Just as you do not believe in equality for women if you are a chauvinist; just as you refuse to accept that all races should have equal standing if you are a racist; just as you cannot be a libertarian if you agree that political suppression is acceptable under certain circumstances, so you should not actively support those who are sexist, racist, dictatorial if you believe in Tolerance. Love them if you do, like them if you wish - but do not encourage or support them in these beliefs or any other of an extreme nature. It returns to Honour (which in itself returns to Truth): what you would not do you should not support others in doing. Tolerate to an extent, but not totally. If someone you love believes or enacts something you hold as being fundamentally wrong, you should tell them so. If they disregard or ignore your feelings and continue in their actions, perhaps you should stop being with them. If they do not respect your fundamental beliefs, they do not respect you.

Part of honour may be respecting someone you disagree with, but if what you disagree with are beliefs and actions that harm others for unreasonable reasons, then that person does not deserve respect. The Pagan creed of 'Do what thou wilt, as long as thou harm none' is applicable to all, Pagan or otherwise. Those who wish to harm for unreasonable reasons (sexism, racism, profit, hatred, abhorrence, etc.) do not deserve respect and they should not be supported. The directive of Tolerance is not a directive to tolerate all; it is a directive to tolerate all that is of an acceptable level. It does not tolerate the unacceptable.

The Six Directives - Truth, Loyalty, Honour, Altruity, Monogamy, Tolerance - can be reduced to their essentials in the following way:

* To be truthful to oneself and others.

* To be loyal to that which merits loyalty.

* To act honourably and recognise others' honour.

* To be generous in one's time and efforts.

* To have an emotional and sexual relationship with only one person at one time.

* To only be intolerant of intolerance.

But this only one code. You may have a different code and approach the living of your life in a different way. Again it comes back to Truth. We must each do what feels right to us. As long as no harm to others comes from it, then what we do, what we believe, the code we hold is a correct one. But whatever directives are held, they should be balanced. Extreme loyalty can be as damaging as false loyalty; to sacrifice oneself too much for others in terms of time, effort or even financially can lead to damaging oneself. All things are relative; we may be extreme at times, but we should not be extreme constantly, as extremism leads to imbalance of the Self and false expectation from others. Once more, it returns to Truth: the truth of knowing what our limits are. To stretch yourself to full magnanimity is good; to pull yourself apart is not. To know this is a recognition that we are merely human; to know we are merely human is to know that we have limitations - and to know that is the first step towards expanding those limitations. To be aware of what we cannot do at present is the base from which we are able to change ourselves so that we *can* do it. It is the foundation from which we can build - and so become more than who we are.

— — —

1 A paradox here: some faiths appear rigid, but are actually quite flexible, while others appear flexible, but

are actually quite rigid. Perhaps it is because some 'rigid' faiths have their flexibility written into their codes and their codes written down, while other 'flexible' faiths do not wish to dictate to their followers and so have little in the way of written codes - thus allowing some followers to conveniently ignore their fundamental principles, but determining others to follow what is written as strictly as it is stated.

2 Unless you genuinely are, in which case you extend an invitation for another time. And if it is a case of not wanting to associate with that person at all, you should have the courage and honesty to say so in whatever way will hurt them least.

3 As to what is the 'appropriate time', individual awareness (or lack of) determines this. The truth can be stated at the wrong time; better this than to state a lie at the right time.

4 There are, as always, exceptions. There are some who would much rather be deceived or live in false hope than to know of a truth which will hurt them. Ignorance can indeed be bliss - but ignorance is one thing, being deluded quite another. An ostrich who puts its head in the sand may be considered foolish; an ostrich whose head has been buried by others has had the choice taken away from them.

5 It is this, more than any other example, that points out the difference between directives and beneficence. Beneficence is beneficent in its intentions; directives are beneficent in their result. A benefaction is decided upon and enacted as each individual situation arises; if that benefaction does not have the intended result, it was not through lack of intention. We meant well even if we did not do well. A directive, though, is a constant. It is an

approach to life; one either applies the directive or one does not. The result shows whether that directive was followed. You are either truthful or you are not, you are either loyal or you are not. . . and so on.

6 This is all very well in theory, of course. The problem comes when it turns out that our lover was not as deserving of altruity as we once thought. How many of us have given much in all kinds of ways, only to discover we were used somewhat after that lover has departed? Perhaps the answer comes from remembering how much was given by our lover when they were there. If there is still a shortfall, at least you gave rather than took. Similarly, if the relationship you are in seems to be decidedly one-sided, then perhaps you should make a careful, considered appraisal of that relationship. Bearing all this in mind, it is hardly surprising that many place progeny above consort in terms of altruity (and indeed, importance) - even though the progeny are often not deserving of it!

7 Walt Whitman: *Song of Myself.*

8 The idea of polygamous relationships may solve certain problems that arise in monogamous partnerships. However, there will always be a fundamental and inescapable flaw in this type of loving. It is a basic human want to be validated, to feel 'special'; any polygamous relationship will constantly be one of imbalance because none of us can share ourselves equally. Though it may be constantly changing, at any given time there will always be one person who is receiving less validation than another and so, no matter how accepting we are of this arrangement, resentment will be there - temporary at first maybe, but temporary resentments become permanent over time.

13.

The Necessity of Pleasure & Pain

Our lives are measured much by the pain and pleasure we feel. The 'perfect moments' we have known, the traumatic events: these are the peaks and troughs of our lifeline. The pleasurable touch and physical injury; the passion and heartbreak; the wisdom and stupidity; the spirit in rapture and despair - all aspects of our Self know pleasure and pain.

Our body is stimulated or revolted; our heart feels love or loss; our head clear or torn in doubt; our spirit ecstatic or overwhelmed by the void. Depression, joy, euphoria, meaninglessness - throughout our lives we are constantly moving into highs and lows.

Pleasure and pain are both positive and negative. Negative pleasure is self-gratification regardless of others; positive pain is when knowledge and understanding is gained through it. To not feel pain is not to learn; to not feel pleasure is not to live. They are the driving forces of our lives. We want to experience one and avoid the other - but to be alive, to truly live, we cannot do this. Pleasure and pain are our measuring stick; they have a symbiotic relationship. We cannot feel one without having felt the other.

To be mutilated or in constant agony may seem too high a price for whatever we gain; to have your heart broken may hurt far more than the love that was felt; to care, to trust and have that care, that trust used and abused may be a betrayal. The pleasure ends so quickly and the pain lasts so long. Life may be unfair - but that is because we only live one life at a time, one moment at a time. We rarely know what is to come, the surprises we may get. We do not know what we will be given in the next life. Certainly we will not care at times; we just want to stop hurting. We usually have that option; we can slice through, rather than shuffle off, this mortal coil.[1] That many of us do not essentially comes down to hope: that things will get better. They may not - but the belief in a faith contains within it the idea that there is a purpose to the events which occur to us. Even if we cannot change our situation ourselves it may be improved for us; and while we are waiting, perhaps there are pleasures still within our grasp. If we do not reach for the fruits, do not bite into them, we lose the chance to taste their sweetness - and often it is the smallest fruits which are the most succulent. The little things often do bring us the most joy.

Pain may be necessary in our lives, but that does not mean we have to accept it with submission. We should not turn the other cheek once we have been struck, but attempt to duck. Part of growth, of balance, of moving towards wholeness is the ability to learn from the mistakes we make. To repeat them time and again, to suffer pain from similar circumstances, is an indication that we need to look into ourselves and change our approach. It shows a tendency we have, an imbalance of the Self. We should have the humility to face that weakness, the wisdom to recognise it for what it is and the courage to try and change it. Our lives are inconsequential enough blips in time and space as it is; the least we should try to do is resonate more fully while living them.

As we learn, grow, move towards balance, we reduce the troughs of our lifeline and multiply the peaks. Perhaps in the lessening of troughs we cannot achieve quite such high peaks; perhaps that is part of our development - by not exposing ourselves to quite so much pain, we reduce our chances of elation. However, this is unlikely. Elation can always be felt. If the heart is open to it, the feeling of love is as exhilarating at eighty as it was at eighteen, if not more so. If the head still pursues it, wisdom, knowledge, understanding still give great satisfaction. The spirit can grow stronger and more peaceful as we grow older. The body may become weak and infirm and crippled, it may be in constant pain, but pleasure is still experienced through the senses - sights that delight the eye, sounds that please the ear, smells and tastes that penetrate. Even the caress can be recognised for what it is, if not felt. And if it is true that elation is not quite so strong, does not last so long, perhaps the lessons we learn from experience keep us more above the median line than below - and if they do not, maybe it is because we did not really learn as much as we thought.

It has been said that life is a series of fairy tales. Not all of life's fairy tales have happy endings, but they can all contain faith and hope. Faith and hope are, in essence, simple things and - whether in pain or pleasure - we should remember that simplicity. The saddest, most painful of lives will have times of joy and should keep living for and looking forward to those times to come. The happiest, most pleasurable of lives will have anguish and agony and should acknowledge them as reminders of how good life can be. What we have, feel and do today may all change tomorrow, for even the most ordered and regular of lives can be altered in an instant. We may think we are in control of the direction we are taking and the speed at which we take it, but the truth is we only have access to some of the controls some of the time. There is a much greater force at work, and if our lives intersect that force, it will send us spinning. What matters here is not what power we have, but how we view our powerlessness: whether in fear and trepidation or with a sense of excitement. For if life is a series of fairy tales, then faith and hope are not its only contents. There is also the adventure.

– – –

1 Though I would not deny anyone the right to take their own life, there is nothing romantic about the act of suicide. It is painful and messy - and your body looks ridiculous afterwards. Having tried it and seen the result from others who succeeded, the real consequence of suicide is the pain and distress felt by those left behind. Furthermore, it is probably not a good idea to shorten your lifespan in terms of rebirth. To be in that state of utter despair is a test; to carry on living when you no longer want to is a brave act. It is self-benefactory; reward will come.

However, in some cases, the question of 'Did they jump or were they pushed' is very relevant indeed. The final choice may have been made by the victim alone; the causal factors which led to that choice may well have gone beyond the victim's control. Sadly, it is a fact that there are good people who die by their own hand due to others' selfish demands. Their very goodness leads to their downfall as they are ripped apart by those feeding off that goodness, leaving them drained and exhausted - and once they feel they have nothing more left to give, they have no reason to continue living.

14.

Primary, Secondary & Tertiary Elements

The Elementalist approach to individuals - the view that the motivations, actions and reactions of all beings stem from a reflection of their internal Elemental make-up - is very simple in theory. However, this simplicity cannot be carried into the empirical world, because individual personalities are not simple. To state that we have a primary Element, an Element which forms the base of our personality, is to state that this base aspect of the Self is very much a reflection of what we are in our natural state. But we are very rarely in a natural state. To act as we truly are only occurs when we feel completely relaxed - when we are on our own or with those we love. In dealing with the world, we have a reluctance to expose our 'real' self. The reason for this is not necessarily fear or self-protection (though this is often the case). Only the young expose themselves completely; as we get older, we learn that social convention does not appreciate this kind of approach. The people who care about us want us to act how we are; those who do not neither want to see. Our primary aspect is also our most primal. Those who do not know us feel uncomfortable when faced with that primal state, to be close to that level of intimacy. If it continues, they ostracise to a degree the person who presents it. Social convention may be wrong here, but as the Turkish proverb says, a big fish cannot know the sea. We cannot directly care about everyone; there are just too many of us and so (possibly to our shame) we would rather not know someone as they truly are when they are not of great importance in our lives.

This initial withholding of our true selves is done by bringing our secondary aspect to the fore. We present the secondary aspect of ourselves to others as much as our primary one in new situations. In so doing, we allow others a glimpse of ourselves whilst at the same time presenting a mask. As some of these people get to know us better - become friends, lovers, etc. - we lower the mask, lessen the use of that secondary aspect and raise the use of our primary one. Those we do not develop a more intimate relationship with continue to see our secondary aspect prominently.

As to our secondary aspect, there seems to be a strong connection between Water, Earth and Air and Air, Earth and Fire. They share a lot of the same characteristics. If Water is our primary Element, for example, then the secondary Element is usually Earth or Air. Similarly, if Air is the primary Element, then any of the other three could be the secondary. But Fire and Water are a relatively rare combination and observation has shown that there seem to be few people who clearly display these two Elements as their primary and secondary ones. Observation and experience have also led to the conclusion that those people whose primary Element does not match their base aspect (e.g. they are Water or heart-based, but seem to be Air or head-based) invariably show signs of a Damaged Self.

In regards to our tertiary Elements - the aspects of our Self we use least, the Elements that influence us little in our choices and decisions and actions and reactions - they are rarely completely dormant. They may well be accessed by others in our role as Core Elementals, for example. That an individual rarely uses the body or Earth side of their personality in living their life does not mean they never use it (even though that use may be sub- or unconscious), and one of the ways in which they do is in an interrelation with someone who activates that Earth side.

As to why we receive the combination of the Elements we do, why there are different hierarchical orders of the Elements in each of us, there are various possible explanations. One of these is astrological. The primary Element, the base of our Self, often also corresponds to our star sign. As said before, the reasons for this are not the same under the belief system described here, but the correlation is an interesting one. Astrology is an age-old art or science, depending on your interpretation, with considerable variation within its field and much addition and refinement over its development. As part of astrology is concerned with the interrelation between character traits and Elements and as the belief system set out here is concerned with the same, there will be parallels between the two.

If we are a mixture of nature and nurture and environment - if the nature of our Selves can be created and altered by these abstract and concrete influences - then why cannot the positions of constellations and our geographic placement at birth also be as influential?

However, Water, Air, Earth and even Fire can be hot or cold. Astrological influence on our Elemental aspects may not be as influential as the 'temperature' of that Element.

Freeze Air and it will turn to Water in the form of ice; ice burns just as Fire does to the touch; heat Earth to a high enough temperature and it turns to liquid and flows like Water; boil Water and it turns to steam, becomes Air. And what is liquid nitrogen if not cold Fire?

The truth is it cannot be known why we are the way we are. Just how much the Elements influence each and every one of us internally as well as externally - how much they are part of our psychological make-up in addition to the affect they have on our empirical senses - is a question which can never be objectively answered. Which is how it should be. Some questions will never have answers given to them that will be agreed upon by all. Theologians put forward their arguments, psychologists put forward others, philosophers other still. To a certain extent, the human race is what it is because we strive to find these answers. The thought processes that have occurred over this type of questioning has led greatly to this structure all around us known as civilisation - and in the end, perhaps the only answers necessary are the ones each of us believe to be the answers. Agreement *per se* is not necessary; just an agreement within oneself.

A personal belief.

Coða

A Líquið Foundation

Relatively little has been written about the spiritual awe felt towards the Elements, the primal forces which I respect as others do their Gods and Goddesses. This was a deliberate decision. I could have spun an alluring web of magic words, created a text which endeavoured to entice others to follow the same path, jumped on the spiritual bandwagon and milked the lost and lonely for a few dollars and possibly a lot more. It has been done before and no doubt will be done again. It isn't so hard. Words are indeed a powerful tool; combine the right ones, deliver them with passion and presence and you will create a cult. We are all looking for answers; find someone who says they have them and it is tempting to believe, as the offer of relief from continual uncertainty is a tempting offer indeed.

However, if there are answers, no one faith has a monopoly on them. Just as all figureheads are equally valid, so are the faiths they are the figureheads of. I am an Elementalist; you are a Wiccan, a Maori, a Jain. As long as the spiritual path we individually follow is one that advocates benefit and negates harm, then no one faith should be put forward as being superior to another. To 'sell' a particular faith or belief system, to look for converts, seems to me to be fundamentally wrong. People should decide what faith to follow independently and of their own accord, not be converted or otherwise pressurized into doing it. And this is why Elementalism, the path set out here, has been described in the manner that it has. There is little in the way of ecstatic spiritual outpourings; no attempt to convert with passages of evangelical fervour; no narration of the personal horrors lived through, the anguish and agony felt, the visions received, the subsequent understanding. I wanted to write about a belief system, not the person who believes it.

As to why it is felt these beliefs deserve to be stated, the primary reason is not because of their possible answering of questions, but rather because they seem relevant and valid in respect to contemporary life. Through agreement or disagreement with them, these beliefs may help in the crystallisation of thought for people who feel somewhat confused both emotionally and spiritually in these confusing times.

For these are confusing times. Families, communities, whole societies are breaking down. Couples are finding it too difficult to stay together and too easy to leave; people are becoming ever more dangerously extreme in their search for a better quality of life or angry and destructive because they have none; nations are struggling with crippling debt, over or under-population in given areas and too few solutions to too many problems. We are becoming lost and directionless, both individually and collectively. Which is no doubt partly why so many of us are yet again this century turning towards a more spiritual approach to the living of our lives.

The truth is that many of us no longer like the world we live in. Pollution of air and water, deforestation, homelessness, poverty, starvation, unemployment, war - we do not want these or many other things that are forced upon us in the name of politics, business, economics or technological growth. We want a cleaner, simpler, better world; a world not like the past, but one that could have been our future if not for greed, selfishness and short-sighted thinking. But there is nothing we can do about it. We have to lock ourselves into a system we hate in order to ensure the survival of what we love: our families, our homes, ourselves. We have to accept what is because none of us can individually change it all - for if we tried, the chances are we would lose everything genuinely precious to us in that attempt and it would be highly doubtful we would succeed. There is no place for a Ghandi anymore; the world has been fragmented far too much.

So if we cannot alter the world or affect the outside, our only choice is to look inside. In a system that is crumbling because the design contained fundamental flaws, we must turn inwards to find our foundations and discover alternatives. By developing the Self, we hope to achieve some sort of peace and make - as Milton put it in his Christian belief - a Heav'n of Hell.[1] And a spiritual belief helps us to do this. It gives form to our personal codes; structure to how we feel we should approach the living of our lives. If religion was once the opium of the people, it is no longer so. It has been replaced by television - releasing it to be what, at heart, it always should have been: a source of balance, comfort and understanding.

And maybe, just maybe, by achieving balance, by finding comfort, by beginning to understand, our collective approach in the world will result in a change *to* the world.

Instead of fighting against the establishment, we simply alter the establishment by no longer asking of it what we once did. Take away the demand and you destroy the power and profit of those who supply.[2] Perhaps a better world will come not from external conflict, but by internal balance.

Just how much the path described in this book achieves this balance; just how much it does provide answers is up to anyone who decides to take the time to contemplate it. The belief system posited here is precisely that: a *belief* system. There is no evidence, no statement to which a finger can be pointed which proves it to be correct. It is not even correct for me. The beliefs I have, the truths I hold, are truths which are constantly ebbing and flowing. The basis of Elementalism is not fixed; it is a liquid foundation rather than a solid one. If a truth is received that requires a change to that foundation, then the constituency of that liquid will be altered. It will be refined, filtered, added to or taken away as I feel directed.[3] But these changes are slowly leading to a solidification. The truth is that I have not got it all figured out just yet. . . but I am getting there.

Yet when I do (or indeed if; for there is no guarantee that anything we strive for will reach completion, no matter how much we wish it), it will still only be truth for me. Your truths have to be felt by yourself, through your own personal quest.

May we all find the grails we are looking for.

– – –

1 John Milton: *Paradise Lost*, Book I.

2 There will always be people who seek power and profit; if the only way they can attain it is by improving the world, then that is how they will do it.

3 Even as this final chapter has been written, there have been changes. The process of writing this text has in itself helped to solidify the belief system. Some of the statements which appear in this book now seem to be too rigid; others not clarified enough. There are points made which are of lesser importance than originally thought; others which have risen to the fore; still others which have not been mentioned at all because there is no awareness of them as yet. Fortunately, a book is not a faith: you can choose when to stop.

Two Years Afterword

Stumbling Through the Undergrowth

Everything you have read so far, with some minor revisions and additions, was written in 1996, when this book appeared under the title '*Elementalism*' and I was writing under the nom de plume of Joseph Madell. Two years have passed since then. Two years is a long time in some ways: we can learn a lot in two years. On a personal level, it would be good to say that in those two years of learning, I have become a wiser, better, more balanced individual and a generally wonderful guy all round. Unfortunately, it would not be true. The fact is in some aspects I have moved forward, but in too many others I have gone backwards. Just because you believe in a set of principles, write them down even, does not mean you always stick to them. That is part of being human, I guess. We strive towards ideals, but more often than not fail to get there. In a way that is a good thing. Imagine a world full of perfect people saying perfect things and doing perfect acts. Does a perfect world sound wonderful to you - or does it sound boring, if for no other reason than the conversation would be really dull? The point is we will always make mistakes; it's repeating the *same* mistakes that we should try to avoid. We are never going to get it right every time, but hopefully, by striving towards the ideal, we will not get it wrong so much. We are never going to be perfect, but by trying as best we can to stick to our beliefs, we hope to become less imperfect.

* * *

Previously in this text, I wrote about the need to step carefully through the undergrowth of life: to take care in respect of what we say or do in relation to avoiding hurt and harm to others (these 'others' not necessarily only being human, but any life force, including Mother Earth herself). The fact is, though, we frequently do not have the *time* to step carefully. Often, we have to make quick decisions about what is the right thing to do; often, we say things before we realise we were going to say them. Who has not, for example, uttered a humorous, vicious one-liner about someone which just popped out of our mouth - and then sat there, moments later, aghast at what we just said?

The truth is almost all of us think we are better than we truly are. We see ourselves in a favourable light. A hard lesson many of us have to learn is that we are nowhere near as good a person as we believe. Many of us advocate the idea of tolerance, for example; the reality is that we can all be very intolerant on occasions. There are certain types of people who get right up our nose; if we interact with them at the wrong time, our tolerance level disappears through the floor. Though tolerance is very important to us as an abstract principle, there comes a time in practice when we realise we are not as tolerant as we believed. However, this is not a case of back to the drawing board, of re-examining the principles; rather that we should actively strive to be tolerant when we are feeling intolerant. In so doing, perhaps we will become as tolerant as we once erroneously thought we were and, indeed, more so.

In the forest of life, we may wish to step carefully through the undergrowth, we may indeed step carefully when we are able to - but more often than not, we are stumbling through it. And perhaps that is as it should be. Better to walk forward in confidence and trip over than to tentatively step, simply because by walking and falling, walking and falling, we reach our destination a lot faster than by safe meandering. Furthermore, tentative steps are of no use when the ground is muddy (and the ground is often muddy). You are going to fall over anyway and the landing is just as painful either way.

But when you're flat on your back in the mud and undergrowth, try to remember this: you may have fallen over this time, but lots of times you haven't. Many of us take our successes lightly and our failures heavily. We dwell on the latter far more than we acknowledge the former. I write these words on my thirty-fifth birthday. I am half-way through my supposed allotted three score years and ten - and if I have a message at thirty-five, the message is this: don't be so hard on yourself. It's a good message to have - clichéd perhaps, but usually something is clichéd because it is true. So, to anyone reading this, here is a present on my birthday to you. Don't be so hard on yourself. Remember the times you got it right.

* * *

As this decade has passed, more and more of us are finding ourselves in an uncomfortable position regarding the society we live in. We are drifting further and further away from the materialistic world of home ownership, career advancement, credit cards and designer labels. Each year we earn less and less, but we also spend less and less. We sometimes think about departing from the 'rat-race', to travel free of worldly concerns beyond that of where the next meal is coming from and trusting in the Powers That Be to look after us. Alternatively, we think about going back to the land to grow our own food and build a house out of wood and stone. These are fantasies, of course. It is more likely to be the welfare state looking after us than the Otherworld and our gardening, let alone building, skills are limited to say the least. But we could become part of the alternative society which once again is a growing force in this and many other countries.

The problem is, we do not fit into the alternative society. There are possessions we enjoy owning; things we like doing that cost money to do. Furthermore, if we have a headache, we do not believe it is because one of our chakras is blocked due to a failure to ground ourselves properly that day with earth energy. We believe we have a headache because the air quality is lousy, we've been working too hard or, more likely, because we had too much to drink last night. So we find ourselves straddling two camps, a foot in each, but a place in neither.

If this sounds even vaguely familiar to you then you are one of the many who, to paraphrase Timothy Leary, turned on, tuned in. . . and got confused. We can hear the music, we feel the rhythm - but we are having real trouble dancing to it. We love the freedom to drive to different places in the cars we own, we want the money to buy the petrol needed to get us there - but we are unsure about the way we are earning that money, feel guilty about the harmful pollutants we leave in our wake and worry about the over-exploitation of this planet's natural resources. To a lesser or greater extent, a great many people are divided between two different ways of living and have ended up somewhere between them both. It is distressing, painful even, to find yourself in this position. It is also how we are meant to be at certain times in our life.

Whatever type of journey life is, it is not a pre-booked holiday. We do not know the destination and we do not always travel there in comfort. Sometimes, there are dangers and fearful situations; sometimes, unexpected delights and pleasant surprises - and sometimes, we have to wait awhile before we cross the border from one country to another. A change in conciousness, in how we approach and live life, *should* be a slow thing. We should get the feeling that we are not sure where we are or where we are going. Without the realisation that we are lost, how would we recognise the place we are looking for when we finally find it?

Only chemicals change instantly; human beings take time to do it. And anyone who says they changed overnight only began to change. To believe otherwise is an illusion.

* * *

Many people now believe in alternative and New Age ideas to varying degrees. Few laugh at the idea of homeopathic remedies any longer, even if they do not use them. In society as a whole, there are more people with a social conscience and a concern for the planet's welfare than ever before. Yet, paradoxically, it now seems that for every failing in character and action there is a New Age excuse - and the biggest excuse of all is the misuse of the phrase 'self-development'.

Self-development is important. This entire book has been written on the basis that we should strive to develop ourselves. But part of the reason why we exist in the world is to contribute something *to* the world: that the world benefits, whether minutely or significantly, from each individual's existence on it. That beneficial contribution from each of us may be greatly intertwined with our personal growth, but our desire for self-development should not be pursued at the cost of our contribution to the world. I am not the most important person on the planet, neither are you and neither is anyone else.

Self-development does not come from a weekend away of therapeutic primal screaming or by buying a huge piece of quartz.[1] Self-development comes from looking at yourself honestly and critically and recognising the positive and negative qualities about yourself. It comes from maintaining those positive qualities and using them to the good of yourself and others; it comes from taking those negative qualities and reducing their influence when acting and interacting in the society we live in. In other words, part of self-development is about admitting when we are wrong or at fault and attempting to ensure we do not make the mistake again. It is not about finding a different type of excuse for our failings.

* * *

It is heartening to see that humanity in general is becomingly increasingly aware of the damage being done to the planet we live on and that active steps are now being taken to stop the destruction. It is worrying to see how small and how slow these steps are. Many of us know that unless drastic action is undertaken soon, it will be too late to do anything at all. The oxygen will still be out there, but our children (and certainly our grand-children) may not be able to breathe it - and even if they can, the world on which they live may not be able to keep them alive. We are running out of natural resources and the unnatural resources we have created are only speeding up the process.

What crime has this planet committed that it should now be moving so inexorably toward execution? What transgressions have the creatures who roam its surface, swim its seas, fly its skies, made to face extinction? What pain have the trees and the plants, the seed and the root, the minerals and the stones, inflicted that they should be punished in this way? And what have the peaceful people, the innocents and the infants, done to deserve the future they will receive?

Within each life we live, we actually live two lives: the life in which we *learn* to live and the life we *then* live. It is in the first that we make most of our mistakes; hopefully in the second, we no longer continue repeating those mistakes. If we do, then natural justice will mete out punishment. However, if there is a natural justice, then it is a natural justice for all forms of life. Just as we can be punished individually for the transgressions we make, so we can be punished as a species - and if the species known as *homo sapiens* continues to flaunt its power and destructive capability over this planet, if we refuse to change the way in which we treat the world, then natural justice will respond in kind - and we will deserve our disappearance as a life force for our apathy.

* * *

Sometimes, we have moments of satori. An event or thought occurs to us which gives us an insight we had not realised previously. We understand something that before was a mystery or enigma. But some events or thoughts are subtler than satori. We do or think of something which seems inconsequential at the time and it is only later we realise that the inconsequentiality was, in fact, very important indeed - and on occasions even momentous.

As we grow older, these moments subtler than satori occur with greater frequency for many of us. Life does not slap us in the face so much anymore. We no longer resist the lessons we need to learn as we once did, so we no longer need to have them hit us on the head so hard. Socrates said many centuries ago that the first step to wisdom is the realisation that you know nothing; perhaps the second step is the realisation that, no matter how much wisdom you gain, it is nothing compared to the wisdom still to be gained. When we are young, we tend to notice voices that are loud; as we grow older perhaps we listen more carefully to a whisper than a shout.

Yet becoming wiser is not simply a matter of growing older. We only become wiser if, no matter how old we are, we continue learning. Hopefully, we will carry on learning until the day we die - and after that, perhaps we really *will* gain wisdom.

* * *

Wisdom and experience; experience and understanding. No matter how wise we are, how experienced we get, how much we understand - when things do not go how we expected them to, we get resentful and angry. Wisdom tells us, for example, that we cannot be open to love unless we are willing to risk pain; experience tells us, though we hope for the best, this will not always occur; understanding tells us that relationships are like trying to find a custom fit in an off-the-peg world.

Yet who has not felt resentful and angry at some point after a love affair is over? It may be true that it is erections, not love, which cannot be sustained - but it is also true that love alone will not keep a relationship alive and sometimes you have to walk away. If you love someone, there will be times of pain. If you love someone, there will be times of compromise and sacrifice. But if the compromises and sacrifices are too many and too frequent; if the pain is too often and too much; if what is given is not balanced to a certain extent by what is received, it is time to quit. You should, of course, talk before you walk. If change is needed, ask for it. If change does not come, or continues to swiftly revert back to how things were despite frequent reminders, then you are justified in leaving. Be a martyr to a cause, to a belief, but never a martyr to love. There is more to life than relationships and if you continue a relationship after its 'sell-by' date, you are doing neither yourself nor your lover a service, no matter how much either of you feel otherwise at the time. You are not meant to be journeying together; continue to do so and you are, in effect, diverting both of you from the journeys you should be on.

This passage about love has been written because the first example given in this book was also about love. Then the point was about how wrong it is to break up a relationship between two people; later it was pointed out how important it is not to give up on a relationship too easily; now the point being made is how important it is to end a relationship when it is bad for you. Wisdom, experience and understanding will not tell you this by themselves, of course; you also need time. Six weeks is not enough to judge; six months may not be enough either; six years is way too long. What wisdom, experience and understanding should tell you is how to do it with as least pain as possible to you both[2] and how to live with it once it is done.

* * *

Some people can sleep through anything because they get so much practice at it while awake. Some people can sleep easily because they are at peace with themselves and the world. I am a heavy sleeper; I am also an insomniac. I reveal this piece of boring information in order to reiterate at the end of this book one of the things said at the very beginning - namely, that everything written here could be complete garbage. I believe I have written truths and that this text is my very small contribution to the world - but I could also be totally missing the point and the approach to the living of life set down here could be completely vacuous.

Perhaps I am sleeping through the real meaning of life and have only an illusion of peace. How we each approach and respond to life should be decided individually. Not by religions, not by gurus, not by leaders, not by friends or family, relatives or lovers - and not by writers of books. Consider what they have to say, by all means; let them influence you if you feel that influ-ence is a positive one - but let the final decisions be made by you alone. It is, after all, your life; how you approach the living of it (for better or worse) affects you most of all.

No matter what happens to you - whether you are imprisoned for a crime you did not commit; born with an affliction that renders you helpless; win the lottery and become an overnight millionaire; gain awards and fame in your chosen profession or live a relatively uneventful life - it is you who has to reconcile what you say and do with yourself. We can indeed escape everything except ourselves, except perhaps through madness (and even the mad were sane once). How we view who we are - whether with pride, sorrow or a mixture of both - is determined by how we approach life, and surely that, if nothing else, should ultimately be decided by ourselves. To let others create false pride or unnecessary sorrow within us must be a mistake, for the first will quickly fade and the second should not be there. No matter how subjective truth may be, the two statements above must be true. Why would we have the cognitive ability to make decisions, if not to decide for ourselves?

The test of a religion, a faith or a philosophy is not to think it, but to live it. I am trying to live mine. I hope you are discovering or creating one which you too can live. If this book has helped, then I have done my job. And if you already have a religion, faith or philosophy which works for you, then hopefully this book made an interesting comparison. Whichever, may the mistakes you make be small and the rewards you receive be bountiful.

Be well, be loved, be happy.

_ _ _

1   Crystal size is rather like penis envy. Having a large one will not necessarily benefit you any more than a small one. Its benefit comes from how it is used, not how big it is. However, having said that, large crystals can have a very powerful influence. Whether the same is true for large penises I would not know!

2   Or all of you, if there are children involved.

FREE CATALOGUE

Capall Bann is owned and run by people actively involved in many of the areas in which we publish. A detailed illustrated catalogue is available on request, SAE or International Postal Coupon appreciated. **Titles can be ordered direct from Capall Bann, post free in the UK** (cheque or PO with order) or from good bookshops and specialist outlets.
Do contact us for details on the latest releases at: **Capall Bann Publishing, Freshfields, Chieveley, Berks, RG20 8TF.** Titles include:

A Breath Behind Time, Terri Hector
Angels and Goddesses - Celtic Christianity & Paganism, M. Howard
Arthur - The Legend Unveiled, C Johnson & E Lung
Astrology The Inner Eye - A Guide in Everyday Language, E Smith
Auguries and Omens - The Magical Lore of Birds, Yvonne Aburrow
Asyniur - Womens Mysteries in the Northern Tradition, S McGrath
Begonnings - Geomancy, Builder's Rites & Electional Astrology in the
 European Tradition, Nigel Pennick Between Earth and Sky, Julia Day
Book of the Veil , Peter Paddon
Caer Sidhe - Celtic Astrology and Astronomy, Vol 1, Michael Bayley
Caer Sidhe - Celtic Astrology and Astronomy, Vol 2 M Bayley
Call of the Horned Piper, Nigel Jackson
Cat's Company, Ann Walker
Celtic Faery Shamanism, Catrin James
Celtic Faery Shamanism - The Wisdom of the Otherworld, Catrin James
Celtic Lore & Druidic Ritual, Rhiannon Ryall
Celtic Sacifice - Pre Christian Ritual & Religion, Marion Pearce
Celtic Saints and the Glastonbury Zodiac, Mary Caine
Circle and the Square, Jack Gale
Compleat Vampyre - The Vampyre Shaman, Nigel Jackson
Creating Form From the Mist - The Wisdom of Women in Celtic Myth and
 Culture, Lynne Sinclair-Wood
Crystal Clear - A Guide to Quartz Crystal, Jennifer Dent
Crystal Doorways, Simon & Sue Lilly
Crossing the Borderlines - Guising, Masking & Ritual Animal Disguise in the
 European Tradition, Nigel Pennick
Dragons of the West, Nigel Pennick
Earth Dance - A Year of Pagan Rituals, Jan Brodie
Earth Harmony - Places of Power, Holiness & Healing, Nigel Pennick

Earth Magic, Margaret McArthur
Eildon Tree (The) Romany Language & Lore, Michael Hoadley
Enchanted Forest - The Magical Lore of Trees, Yvonne Aburrow
Eternal Priestess, Sage Weston
Eternally Yours Faithfully, Roy Radford & Evelyn Gregory
Everything You Always Wanted To Know About Your Body, But So Far
    Nobody's Been Able To Tell You, Chris Thomas & D Baker
Face of the Deep - Healing Body & Soul, Penny Allen
Fairies in the Irish Tradition, Molly Gowen
Familiars - Animal Powers of Britain, Anna Franklin
Fool's First Steps, (The) Chris Thomas
Forest Paths - Tree Divination, Brian Harrison, Ill. S. Rouse
From Past to Future Life, Dr Roger Webber
God Year, The, Nigel Pennick & Helen Field
Goddess on the Cross, Dr George Young
Goddess Year, The, Nigel Pennick & Helen Field
Goddesses, Guardians & Groves, Jack Gale
Handbook For Pagan Healers, Liz Joan
Handbook of Fairies, Ronan Coghlan
Healing Book, The, Chris Thomas and Diane Baker
Healing Homes, Jennifer Dent
Healing Journeys, Paul Williamson
Healing Stones, Sue Philips
Herb Craft - Shamanic & Ritual Use of Herbs, Lavender & Franklin
Hidden Heritage - Exploring Ancient Essex, Terry Johnson
Hub of the Wheel, Skytoucher
In Search of Herne the Hunter, Eric Fitch
Inner Celtia, Alan Richardson & David Annwn
Inner Mysteries of the Goths, Nigel Pennick
Inner Space Workbook - Develop Thru Tarot, C Summers & J Vayne
Intuitive Journey, Ann Walker
Isis - African Queen, Akkadia Ford
Journey Home, The, Chris Thomas
Kecks, Keddles & Kesh - Celtic Lang & The Cog Almanac, Bayley
Language of the Psycards, Berenice
Legend of Robin Hood, The, Richard Rutherford-Moore
Lid Off the Cauldron, Patricia Crowther
Light From the Shadows - Modern Traditional Witchcraft, Gwyn
Living Tarot, Ann Walker
Lore of the Sacred Horse, Marion Davies
Lost Lands & Sunken Cities (2nd ed.), Nigel Pennick
Magic of Herbs - A Complete Home Herbal, Rhiannon Ryall

Magical Guardians - Exploring the Spirit and Nature of Trees, Philip Heselton
Magical History of the Horse, Janet Farrar & Virginia Russell
Magical Lore of Animals, Yvonne Aburrow
Magical Lore of Cats, Marion Davies
Magical Lore of Herbs, Marion Davies
Magick Without Peers, Ariadne Rainbird & David Rankine
Masks of Misrule - Horned God & His Cult in Europe, Nigel Jackson
Medicine For The Coming Age, Lisa Sand MD
Medium Rare - Reminiscences of a Clairvoyant, Muriel Renard
Menopause and the Emotions, Kathleen I Macpherson
Mind Massage - 60 Creative Visualisations, Marlene Maundrill
Mirrors of Magic - Evoking the Spirit of the Dewponds, P Heselton
Moon Mysteries, Jan Brodie
Mysteries of the Runes, Michael Howard
Mystic Life of Animals, Ann Walker
New Celtic Oracle The, Nigel Pennick & Nigel Jackson
Oracle of Geomancy, Nigel Pennick
Pagan Feasts - Seasonal Food for the 8 Festivals, Franklin & Phillips
Patchwork of Magic - Living in a Pagan World, Julia Day
Pathworking - A Practical Book of Guided Meditations, Pete Jennings
Personal Power, Anna Franklin
Pickingill Papers - The Origins of Gardnerian Wicca, Bill Liddell
Pillars of Tubal Cain, Nigel Jackson
Places of Pilgrimage and Healing, Adrian Cooper
Practical Divining, Richard Foord
Practical Meditation, Steve Hounsome
Practical Spirituality, Steve Hounsome
Psychic Self Defence - Real Solutions, Jan Brodie
Real Fairies, David Tame
Reality - How It Works & Why It Mostly Doesn't, Rik Dent
Romany Tapestry, Michael Houghton
Runic Astrology, Nigel Pennick
Sacred Animals, Gordon MacLellan
Sacred Celtic Animals, Marion Davies, Ill. Simon Rouse
Sacred Dorset - On the Path of the Dragon, Peter Knight
Sacred Grove - The Mysteries of the Forest, Yvonne Aburrow
Sacred Geometry, Nigel Pennick
Sacred Nature, Ancient Wisdom & Modern Meanings, A Cooper
Sacred Ring - Pagan Origins of British Folk Festivals, M. Howard
Season of Sorcery - On Becoming a Wisewoman, Poppy Palin
Seasonal Magic - Diary of a Village Witch, Paddy Slade
Secret Places of the Goddess, Philip Heselton

Syncretis & Elementalism } P 56 - 65

Secret Signs & Sigils, Nigel Pennick
Self Enlightenment, Mayan O'Brien
Shamanica, Martine Ashe
Spirits of the Air, Jaq D Hawkins
Spirits of the Earth, Jaq D Hawkins
Spirits of the Fire, Jaq D Hawkins
Stony Gaze, Investigating Celtic Heads John Billingsley
Stumbling Through the Undergrowth , Mark Kirwan-Heyhoe
Subterranean Kingdom, The, revised 2nd ed, Nigel Pennick
Symbols of Ancient Gods, Rhiannon Ryall
Talking to the Earth, Gordon MacLellan
Taming the Wolf - Full Moon Meditations, Steve Hounsome
Teachings of the Wisewomen, Rhiannon Ryall
The Other Kingdoms Speak, Helena Hawley
Tree: Essence of Healing, Simon & Sue Lilly
Tree: Essence, Spirit & Teacher, Simon & Sue Lilly
Through the Veil, Peter Paddon
Torch and the Spear, Patrick Regan
Understanding Chaos Magic, Jaq D Hawkins
Vortex - The End of History, Mary Russell
Warp and Weft - In Search of the I-Ching, William de Fancourt
Warriors at the Edge of Time, Jan Fry
Water Witches, Tony Steele
Way of the Magus, Michael Howard
Weaving a Web of Magic, Rhiannon Ryall
West Country Wicca, Rhiannon Ryall
Wildwitch - The Craft of the Natural Psychic, Poppy Palin
Wildwood King , Philip Kane
Witches of Oz, Matthew & Julia Philips
Wondrous Land - The Faery Faith of Ireland by Dr Kay Mullin
Working With the Merlin, Geoff Hughes
Your Talking Pet, Ann Walker
Menopausal Woman on the Run, Jaki da Costa

Environmental
Gardening For Wildlife Ron Wilson

FREE CATALOGUE

Capall Bann Publishing, Freshfields, Chieveley, Berks, RG20 8TF.